It's not what you hurl, but *The Hurl* itself that matters.

The Big Book of Catapult and Trebuchet PLANS!

By Ron L. Toms

Published by RLT Industries, Inc.
www.RLT.com

Published by RLT Industries, Inc.

For more information, visit http://www.RLT.com

ISBN 978-0-9776497-3-0

Printed in the United States of America

CONTENTS

Section One
Getting Prepared

Section Two
The Trebuchets

Section Three
Torsion and Tension Machines

Section Four
Going Farther

Author's preface

This book is a collection of plans for various catapult projects that I have developed over the course of a decade. The styles of the drawings are not consistent, and I apologize for that. As the software at my disposal changed, my skills and objectives changed, and occasionally the drawings were outsourced to hired help, the quality and style of the drawings varied dramatically. Also, some of the original files have been lost -- I've suffered through more than one complete hard drive failure over the years -- so in at least one case the images were extracted from a low resolution PDF file. But all the necessary information should be there, even if they are not the most elegant pages to read.

At one time, every model in this book was being manufactured in my small warehouse and sold in kit form over the Internet. They have been extremely popular as middle-school and high-school science projects, and we've even sold a few for PHD thesis work in both history and higher mathematics, the latter being a study in chaotic motion of a double ended pendulum, which is exactly what a hanging-counterweight trebuchet is. The smooth, almost poetic launch sequence usually becomes chaotic just after the projectile is released.

From simple concepts like "heavier things don't go as far", to more complex relationships of arm and sling ratios, projectile/counterweight ratios, optimizing arm fulcrum points and exploring chaos theory, there are a myriad of lessons that can be learned in science, engineering and history from these machines. These models have also been popular with corporate team building workshops, summer camps, and hobbyists of all ages for building social and mechanical skills too.

But by far, the biggest demand for these models has been from people involved in school science projects. Whether in a classroom or homeschool, the educational potential for a catapult project is enormous. I hope that this book helps to make it more accessible to parents and teachers alike. Be sure to read the sections at the end of this book for more information about the educational utility of kit building, and the Floating Arm Trebuchet instructions include a math lesson (pg. 44) for calculating efficiency and range optimization.

Manufacturing the models in this book are how I made my living for most of a decade. As such, I took their designs very seriously, often going through a dozen iterations before settling on the final design. They were designed to work, and to work well. However, you may still be able to improve on them without too much difficulty. The design process I used included considerations for manufacturing large volumes of kits, making them easy to build for the average person, minimizing the cost, and efficient shipping. You won't be limited by those constraints!

Still, it always surprises me that people think they have to ask my permission to change something in these plans or in a kit they've purchased from me. Remember folks, if you bought it, you can do whatever you want with it -- as long as you don't break any laws, that is. And try to be safe about it too. Don't do anything foolish. Getting hurt is a lesson we'd all rather avoid.

-- Ron L. Toms
December, 2010

Section One:
Getting prepared

NOTES ON SAFETY AND WORKING WITH WOOD:

Please read this important notice before you begin building.

Wood is a funny material. It's a product of nature, and as such, it can be a little bit unpredictable. Experienced carpenters say you never know how strong a piece of wood is until it breaks. **We strongly agree.**

We strongly advise that you use a good, strong wood for your models. Be sure to look for any defects in the wood, such as: knots, checks, cracks, worm-holes or evidence of other wood-boring insects, water damage, etc. DO NOT USE any pieces that have any defects, make a new piece instead. Also, it's important to be aware that any piece of wood can look perfectly fine and apparently free from defects, but may still have faults such as internal stresses, voids and fractures that cannot be seen on its surface.

Ultimately, you are building these models AT YOUR OWN RISK. If you are not qualified to use the tools required, nor to select appropriate pieces of wood to use, we recommend you seek out qualified professional help -- an experienced carpenter, cabinetmaker, mechanical engineer or other suitable expert.

We have taken every reasonable precaution in designing these models, but we cannot be responsible for your choices in wood, how you make the pieces, how you assemble the kit, or how you use it. While we've never had a problem with the kits we've made, we cannot make the same assurance with one that you might make.

By building a model based on these plans, you agree that you are doing so at your own risk, and that you will not hold RLT Industries or any of its employees or principles liable for any damages or injuries that may occur as a result of the construction or use of this model.

Please be thoughtful and cautious as you proceed, make a plan, pay attention and follow all safety instructions for any and all tools you use.

TOOLS AND TECHNIQUES

"What tools do I need?"   My favorite response to this question, as seen on a an on-line woodworking message board is: "Give a hopeless amateur a world class workshop and the best materials money can buy, and any chair he builds will still wobble. But give a master craftsman a hammer, a chisel and a pile of scrap wood, and he'll turn out a chair that will be strong, sturdy, beautiful and will last a lifetime."

Ultimately, the tools you need will depend on your skills, your comfort level, your budget and how fast you want to work. To design and build the models in this book, we used an ordinary table saw, drill press, miter saw and a portable planer. All of these tools were purchased at a local home improvement store for under $1000 total. Half that was for the planer, which is completely optional. We used it to guarantee dimensional accuracy of the wood and to give it a nice smooth surface on all sides, with sharp corners. But if you're careful and accurate with a table saw, you won't need a planer, and a hand drill can replace the drill press, and if you're really good at using a table saw, you won't need a miter saw at all.

Other tools that would be helpful to have are a bench sander, a bandsaw, and lots and lots of clamps.

Keep in mind that you don't have to build the models exactly as depicted in this book. The ancients used tools that weren't much different from a hammer and chisel, and they made trebuchets large enough to hurl dead horses over castle walls. So be creative and use good judgement about the tools you use. But in any case, always, always follow all the manufacturer's safety notes for the tools you use.

HISTORICAL NOTES ABOUT CATAPULTS:

First of all, don't be confused by the word "catapult". A trebuchet is also a kind of catapult. There are many types of Catapult. In modern times, the word catapult can be used to describe any machine that hurls a projectile. This can include a slingshot used to hurl pebbles, a machine that launches airplanes off aircraft carriers, and of course, the ancient weapons of smash destruction! There are many different kinds of ancient catapults. The three major types are the Ballista, Onager and Trebuchet.

The word "Trebuchet" is originally French, and meant something like "to fall over or rotate about the middle" as in a see-saw rotating on its axle. It also seems to have meant a big, heavy beam. Today a Trebuchet is any kind of catapult that is powered by a massive counterweight on one end of an arm, and a sling on the other end. This includes Perriers, or "traction" trebuchets which are powered by a mass of people pulling one end of the arm with ropes.

The Trebuchet is probably the oldest type of catapult. It was invented either by the Chinese or in the middle east. If you look at an Egyptian shadouf, it looks very much like a trebuchet, and it's easy to imagine that the trebuchet was inspired by the shadouf. Shadoufs have been around since the beginning of recorded history.

A shadouf is just a long pole balanced in the middle, with a weight on one end and a rope attached to the other end with a bucket tied to it. It's easier to pull something down that to lift it up, so people use these shadoufs to lift water from irrigation trenches. (They pull the rope down, and the counterweight pulls the bucket full of water up.) If someone had slipped and let go of the rope, an empty bucket could be flung high and far by the counterweight. A clever person might see the weapons potential in this.
Trebuchets were used mainly as lobbing machines to spread fire and diseased corpses, as well as a lot of solid missiles, over the walls of castles to rain down on the inhabitants. They were very effective!

The next oldest type of catapult is the Ballista. This is a two-armed torsion device invented by the Greeks around 800 BCE. It works similar to a crossbow, but instead of a flexible bow, it uses two stiff arms powered by twisted rope skeins like an Onager. The Ballista predates the Onager by several centuries and was used to hurl stones (Lithobolos style ballista) and also bolts or darts. Obviously, this is where we get the word "ballistic". Variations of the ballista were sometimes called "scorpion"

The Romans took the ballista, used it, and then improved in in the Roman way to create the Scorpion, and then the Onager. Onager is originally the name for the wild Asian donkey. This donkey bucks like a bronco if anyone gets too close to it, and it is known to kick stones at people and predators too. So when the Romans needed a name for their one-armed torsion catapult, they called it the Onager! The Onager has a single arm that is powered by a large skein of twisted ropes. The ropes were usually made from hair or sinew for their elastic properties.

Onagers were used right up to the middle ages alongside the Trebuchet, when gunpowder and the Cannon were invented and eventually replaced the catapults.

In some cultures the Onager was called a Mangonel. The word Mangonel derives from the ancient Greek word "Manganon", literally meaning "engine of war". The Romans called it a Manganum. In pre-medieval French the word Manganum was changed to

Manganeau, and the English changed that to Mangonel in the 1300s. The history gets a little sketchy in the middle ages, but some historians believe that "mangonel" was shortened to the word "gonnel" about the same time that cannons were being developed, and later still, "gonnel" was shortened to "gun." And today, in the military a "gun" is strictly a piece of big artillery, not something an average soldier can carry as a personal firearm.

HOW TO CHOOSE YOUR WEAPON

It really just boils down to two questions-
1. What do you want to hurl, and
2. How far.

The Trebuchet is like a truck- it can haul a heavy load, but it is limited in how far it can hurl it or how easily it can be aimed. The Ballista is like an expensive sports car - easy to aim, stylish and complex to engineer, and limited in payload capacity. Either smallish round stones for the Lithobolos ballista, or bolts (darts) for the more traditional type. The Onager is more like an SUV - it has the power to get a better range than a trebuchet and covers the middle ground for kinds of projectiles you can hurl.

Of course, this all depends on the scale of machine you want to build too. For flinging golf balls and tennis balls, any of these designs will do the job. But if you're going to be hurling bowling balls the length of a football field, I suggest you consult with a good professional engineer (and possibly an insurance agent too).

NOTES ON SCALING:

A lot of people make bad mistakes when trying to scale a model to different sizes. They'll take a set of plans and double or triple the length of all the pieces, then wonder why it all fell apart the first time they tried to cock it.

We'll touch on the fundamentals of scaling, but this is not a comprehensive treatment of the subject. Ultimately, when you scale the model to a significantly different size, it becomes a new design and should be re-engineered from the ground up. However, small changes, especially when scaling down, should be fine if you keep these rules in mind.

Length

This is the easy one. If you have a measurement four feet long, and you want to double it's size (increase its scale a factor of two) then it will be eight feet long. A one foot measurement, scaled up three times, will be three feet long. Scaling a 4 foot measurement to ¼ scale will make it one foot long. And so on. Simple, right?

What a lot of people forget is that they have to scale it in all three dimensions. So, if you have a board that is 2 inches by 4 inches by 8 feet long, and you want it half scale, then you have to cut it to 1 inch by 2 inches by 4 feet. I've seen a lot of people just cut a 2x4 in half and think they are done. If you're doubling the scale of your board, you can't just get a 16 foot 2x4 either. You need a 16 foot board that is 4 inches thick by 8 inches wide, and those are a little harder to find. Doubling the dimensions also has an interesting affect on the weight and strength of a beam.

Mass / Weight

This one loses a lot of people, but once you "get it" it will become obvious -- First of all, mass and weight are not the same thing. But they scale similarly, so don't worry about it. Mass and weight DO NOT scale the same as length though! Too many people make the mistake that if they double the length, then all the weights double too. Not so.

Think about a cube that is one foot by one foot by one foot in length on each side. Its total volume is one cubic foot. Now let's double its scale to 2 feet by 2 feet by 2 feet. Its volume is 2 x 2 x 2, or 8 cubic feet. So, what's obvious here is that the length doubled, but the volume increased by a factor of eight! If we tripled the scale of that one foot cube to 3 feet by 3 feet by 3 feet, then it's volume would be 3 x 3 x 3 = 27 cubic feet! The volume is 27 times as much even though the length only went up three times!

Volume is related to the weight in a one-to-one relationship. The weight per cubic foot of something, times the number of cubic feet you have, equals the weight of the whole thing.

Mass (or weight) scales as the cube of the length. So, if you want to quadruple (four times) the size of a machine, then its weight needs to increase by (4 x 4 x 4 = 64 !!!) 4 cubed = 64 times as much. Scale it up five times, and the weight goes up 125 times. Obviously, your machine is going to have to be a lot stronger to support it's own weight! So let's talk about scaling strength

Strength

Here's where people get into real and serious trouble. When you scale a machine up, say four times, the weight of each member will go up sixty-four times. The mechanical properties of the specific material (shear strength, tensile strength, bending resistance, etc.) haven't changed, and the beam has to support its own weight in addition to the increased weight of any other members that it supports. The result is that the total strength of the machine gets proportionally weaker as the scale goes up.

Strength usually scales as a smaller-than-one fraction of the length.
Fractions smaller than one: 1/2, 1/4, 2/3…
Fractions larger than one: 3/2, 4/3…

The problem is, we don't know what fraction to use unless we know the specific properties of the material and how it's being used. Things like compression, tension, flex, shear, and tear can all scale very differently from each other, even in the same beam or sheet of material.

What does this mean? Basically, when you scale things up, they become relatively weaker. They have more trouble supporting their own weight, and the weight of everything else it supports is also increasing cubically, so at some point you have to change the design, or use materials that are inherently stronger to begin with, and keep their limits in mind too.

Non-scalables

There are things that you can't scale, like gravity. Unless you're wiling to go to the Moon or Mars, etc.

Friction is a product of the frictional coefficient (which is non-scaleable) times surface area (scales as the square of the length) times pressure (uh…). There are whole college courses spent dealing with these issues. It's a little beyond the scope of this introduction, and could be a whole book in itself.

Also, density doesn't scale. So, air resistance (a product of air density and cross sectional area and velocity) isn't easy to scale either. All these things can affect performance, so if you have a catapult that hurls 200 feet, and you double the scale, don't expect it to hurl 400 feet (unless your projectile is considerably less than 8x the weight). Try to figure out more scaling problems on your own. This is a great project for experimentation!

Section Two:
The Trebuchets

1. The PVC Trebuchet Project.

Parts List:

3/4 inch diameter tubing:

2) long base pieces	24"
2) cross base pieces	5 1/2"
8) short connecting pieces	2"
4) angle struts	16-3/4"
2) short arm pieces	7"
1) counterweight stub	2-7/8"

1/2 inch diameter tubing:

1) main axle	4"
1) long arm piece	20"

Connectors (all connectors are the "slip" type unless otherwise noted):
- 1) ½" end cap
- 8) ¾" T connectors
- 4) ¾" 45 degree angle (actually it's 135 degrees, but it's called a 45)
- 2) ¾" elbow with threaded side-outlet
- 2) ½" slip to ½" threaded adaptor
- 1) ¾" cross connector
- 2) ¾" coupler
- 1) ¾" to ½" reducer plug
- 4) ¾" plugs with a small hole drilled in it.

Other parts:
- 2) counterweight disks
- 1) sling twine, about 5 feet.
- 1) burlap pouch material
- 1) square-bend hook 1-13/16" for the release pin
- 1) heavy-duty paper clip for the trigger

Wheels:
- 4) 3 inch wheels.
- 2) ¼" x 12" all-thread bolts
- 4) nuts and washers for the bolts.

Tools and Materials Required:
Pliers or wrench, Scissors, Ruler or tape measure,
Glue (PVC glue, Gorilla Glue, or any plastic glue will work),
Paint (optional)

Assembly Instructions:

All pieces can slip snugly together. For added strength, use any good plastic glue to bond them permanently together. The arm must be glued together or it may fall apart when firing.

1. Sides.

   There are two sides to be constructed.

   Find the two long pieces of 3/4 inch tubing ('A', 24 inches long) and to each end attach a T connector ('B') at the center opening of the T. The connectors must be parallel to each other so that the assembled pieces lay flat.

   Insert a short connecting piece ('C', 2 inches long) into one end of each of the T connectors.

   Set those aside for the moment. Find one of the 90 degree elbows ('D') with threaded side-hole. Insert two of the 16-3/4" struts ('E') into the elbow, and attach two of the 135 degree elbows ('F') to the other ends of these tubes so that the whole assembly lays flat. Repeat with the other pieces.

   Now attach these assemblies by attaching the 135 degree elbows to the short connecting pieces on the base units you previously set aside. You should now have two complete triangles with threaded connectors at the top corners.

   Find the threaded plugs ('G'). These need to be screwed completely into the side-out elbows ('D') so that there are no threads showing. This may be hard to do, so try greasing the threads with Vaseline or Crisco cooking grease. If that doesn't work, use a hacksaw to cut off a few threads until you can screw them all the way in.

2. Base and Wheels.

   Now slide two T connectors ('J') onto each of the 5 1/2 inch tubes. Assemble the frame you constructed previously onto the base pieces by using 2-inch connector pieces into the T connectors.

   Insert the long threaded rod through the base sections, and a plug (with hole) onto the threaded rod. Seat the plug all the way into the pipe.

   Put a wheel over each end of the bolt, and put a washer on the outside of the wheel and secure with a nut, but loosely so that the wheel turns freely. The hub of the wheel should fit just inside the T-fitting. You can lock the nut in place with a drop or two of crazy glue on the threads.

   For the floor of the frame, lay a cardboard strip across the base beams in the center of the machine. The box it shipped in is good for this. Just cut one side out of the shipping box and use the box as a trough.

   You should now have a completed frame!

3. The arm.

Be sure to glue all pieces of the arm together so it doesn't fall apart when you try to fire the machine!

Take the two short arm pieces (7 inches) and insert them into each open end of the cross piece ('H').

Each end of the arm gets a straight coupler ('L') attached to it, and then the 3/4 to 1/2 inch reducer plug ('M') goes into one end, the other end gets the 2-7/8" counterweight stub.

Now screw the square-bend hook screw into the hole in the cap on the long piece. It should be screwed all the way in. The threads of the screw should come out of the opposite side of the arm a little bit. The hook will be under stress when firing, so it needs as much support as possible. The hook MUST be pointing up towards the middle of the arm at a 45-degree angle.

Insert the other end of the tubing onto the reducer plug so that the hook on the end of the arm is perpendicular (points up) when the cross is flat on the table.

Slide the counterweight disks onto the stub at the other end of the arm, and then glue the cap onto the end of the stub.

Now make a sling. Cut a piece of burlap 3 inches by 8 inches (or 6 inches by 8 inches if you want it double thickness). Bunch-up one end of the burlap so that you form a cup shape, and tie it tightly with one end of twine. Make this piece of twine 30 inches long. Do the same thing to the other end of the burlap pouch.

Tie one end of the sling to the hook, and secure it to the arm by tying another short piece of string around the arm just below the cap. You can use a dab of glue to keep these together.

Tie a loop into the other end of the sling. The loop should be about 1/4 to 1/2 inch in diameter so that it can slide off the hook easily. The total length of the sling is measured from the bottom of the pouch to the loops at the end of the twine. It should be about 24 to 26 inches long.

Now get the axle. This is a 1/2 inch diameter tube 4 inches long. Insert this through the cross, and each end of it should go all the way into each of the plugs at the top of the frame. It's not a bad idea to glue the ends of the axle in place, but the cross MUST be able to spin freely on the axle.

4. The trigger.

If you want to have a trigger release, pull the arm down into the cocked position and tie a piece of twine to one side of the frame so that it lays over the arm, and tie a loop in the twine near the other side of the base. Tie another piece of twine to that side of the base, and tie a heavy-duty paperclip to that. Open the paperclip so that it makes a hook, and hook the two pieces of twine together over the arm.

Tie another piece of twine to the paperclip hook, and pull it to release the loop, and thus release the arm.

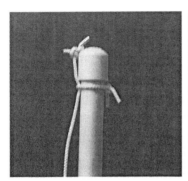  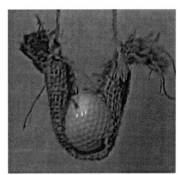

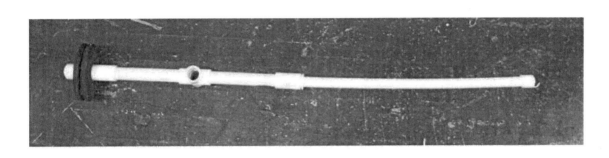

Experiments and tuning tips:

There are lots of things that affect the range you can get with your trebuchet. The first thing people usually think is that "more counterweight means more distance". This is wrong, and can even lead to the projectile being thrown backwards or straight up! Tuning one of these is a little tricky.

The easiest thing to tune is the length of the sling. A too short sling will cause the projectile to shoot too high, and a long sling will make it shoot too low, and hit the ground too soon. The sling should be about as long as the arm is from the pin to the axle, or somewhat shorter. The ratio of the counterweight to the projectile weight, and the ratio of the short end of the arm to the long end of the arm will all have an effect on the proper sling length.

Another way to tune the trebuchet is with the angle of the release pin. If the trebuchet is releasing too early, bend the pin up past 45 degrees. If it's releasing too late, bend it down a bit. It's best to get the sling length right before changing the pin angle.

You can also adjust the proportion of counterweight to projectile. This will depend on the axle position and length of the arm, as well as the height of the axle. For this model, an 80 to 1 counterweight to projectile ratio works pretty well. Try other ratios and see what happens.

With careful tuning of all these parameters, we were able to toss a golf ball 35 feet using a 5 lb counterweight!

Good luck, and have fun!

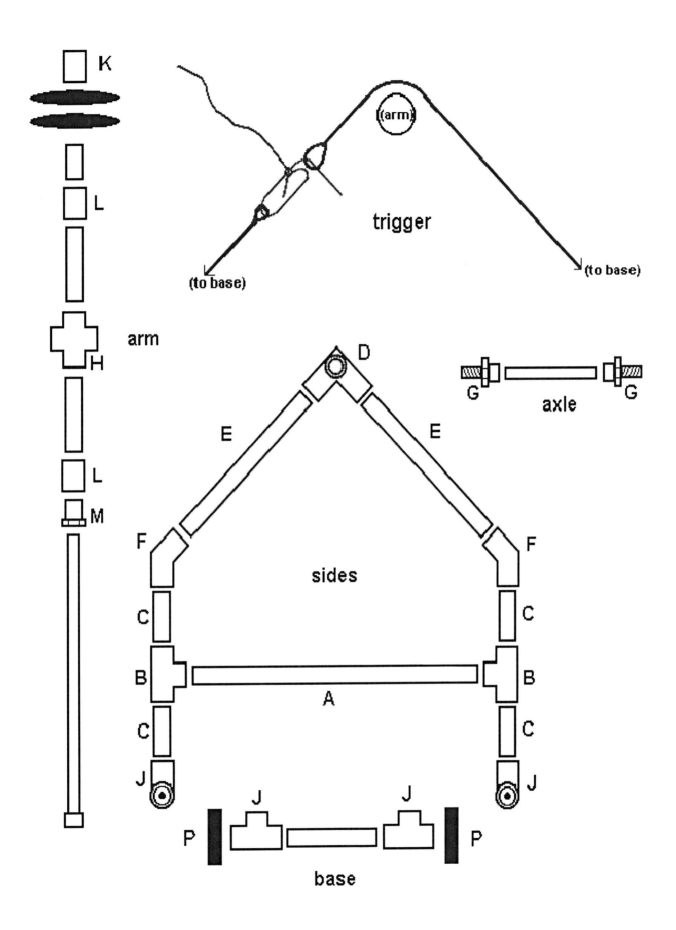

K

L

arm

H

L

M

trigger

(to base)

(to base)

axle

G   G

D

E   E

sides

F   F

C   C

B   B

A

C   C

J   J

J   J

P   P

base

The Tabletop Trebuchet Project:
Parts and Assembly instructions

Misc. parts list:

6 small dowel pegs	3 feet of twine	1 steel looped pin
1 metal pin	1 iron missile	1 pouch (flat)
1 steel ring	3 eye screws	1 wooden ball

Wooden parts you will make:

1 arm 16" long.	1 floor beam 4 ¼" long
2 arm reinforcing pieces	4 brace blocks 1 7/8" long
3 counterweight hangers	2 floor beams 5 ¼" long
3 counterweight pegs	2 base beams 13 ½" long
1 6 ½" axle dowel	2 trough beams 13 ½" long
2 vertical struts 9" long	2 axle dowels 8" long
4 diagonal struts 9 ½" long	4 wooden wheels
2 side braces 6" long	2 angled brace blocks 4" long

Tools you will need:

1. A carpenter's square, or any good 90 degree reference (such as a CD jewel case).
2. A ruler or tape measure.
3. A good wood glue. (Elmer's wood glue is recommended)
4. Two clamps capable of spanning 7 inches.

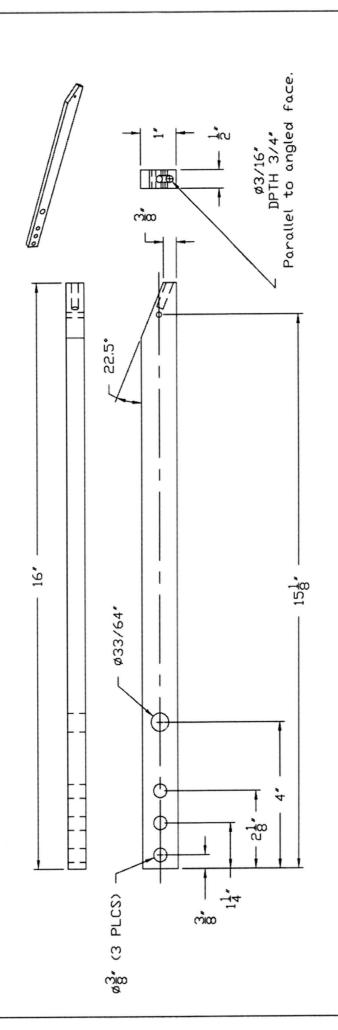

ø3/16"
DPTH 3/4"
Parallel to angled face.

1"

1/2"

3/8"

16"

22.5°

15 1/8"

ø33/64"

4"

2 1/8"

ø3/8" (3 PLCS)

3/8"

1 1/4"

RLT.COM, Inc.

PART NO. TK-1

DWG APRV:

DWG NO. Table Top Treb

REV
A

SHEET

TOLERANCE: Unless noted all
tolerances are ± 1/64. Angles ±3°

Material:

SCALE NONE

DWG BY: RRG

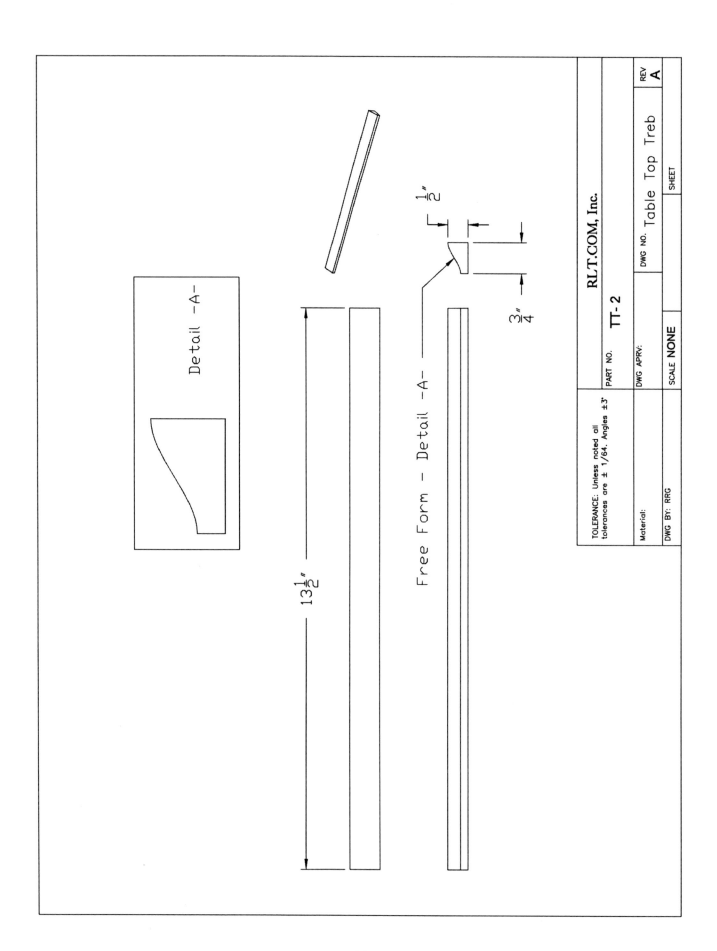

Detail -A-

Free Form - Detail -A-

$13\frac{1}{2}''$

$\frac{1}{2}''$

$\frac{3}{4}''$

RLT.COM, Inc.

TOLERANCE: Unless noted all tolerances are ± 1/64. Angles ±3°			
	PART NO.		
Material:	DWG APRV:	DWG NO. Table Top Treb	REV A
DWG BY: RRG	SCALE NONE	SHEET	

PART NO. TT-2

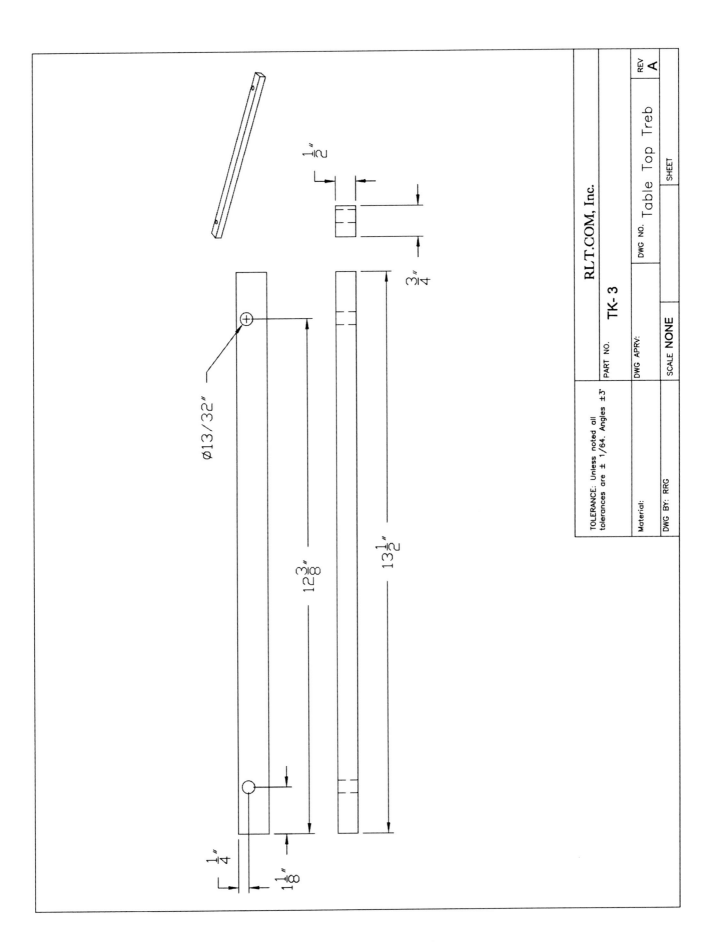

Ø13/32"

12 3/8"

13 1/2"

1/4"

1 1/8"

1/2"

3/4"

RLT.COM, Inc.

TOLERANCE: Unless noted all tolerances are ± 1/64. Angles ±3°

PART NO. TK-3

DWG NO. Table Top Treb

REV A

Material:

DWG APRV:

DWG BY: RRG

SCALE NONE

SHEET

16

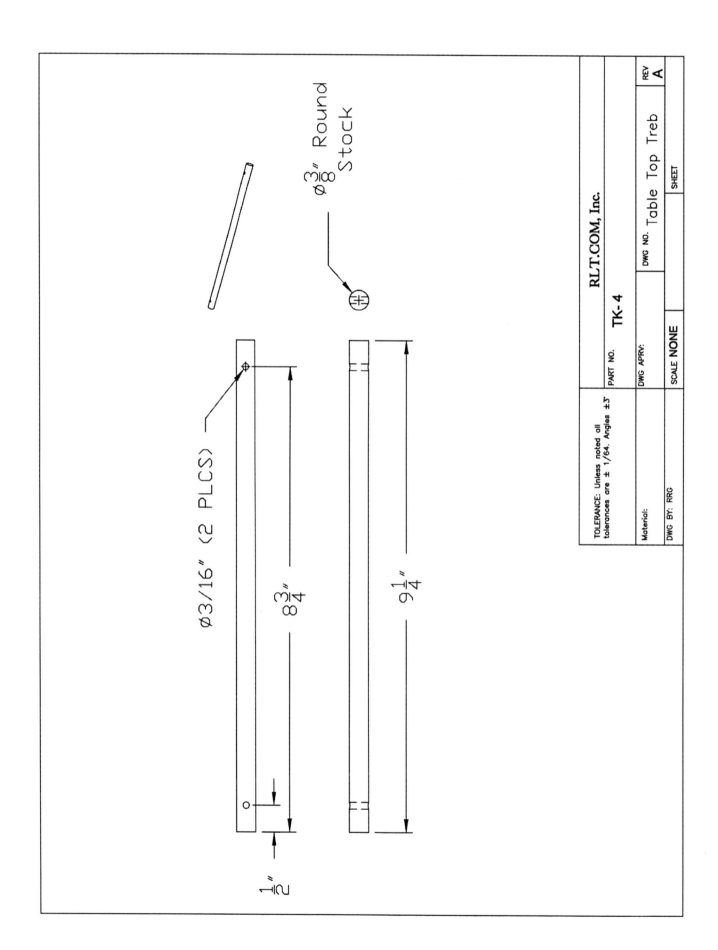

Ø3/8" Round Stock

Ø3/16" (2 PLCS)

8 3/4"

9 1/4"

1/2"

RLT.COM, Inc.

TOLERANCE: Unless noted all tolerances are ± 1/64. Angles ±3°

PART NO. TK-4

DWG NO. Table Top Treb

REV A

Material:

DWG APRV:

SCALE NONE

SHEET

DWG BY: RRG

17

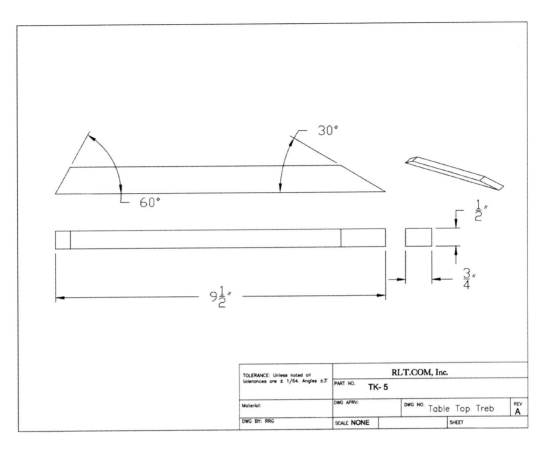

30°

60°

9½"

½"

¾"

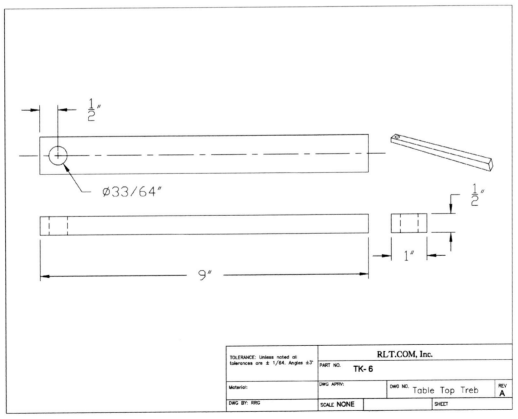

½"

Ø33/64"

9"

½"

1"

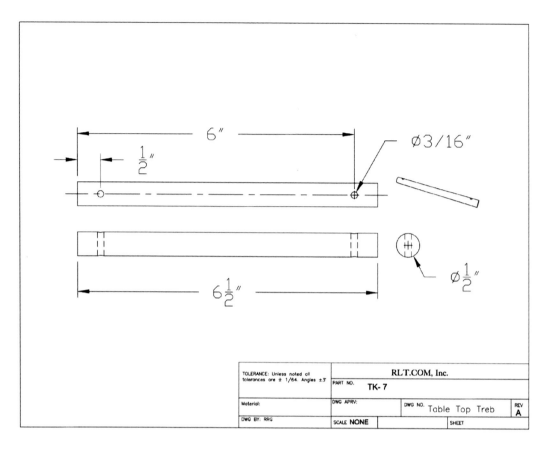

6"

½"

Ø3/16"

6½"

Ø½"

TOLERANCE: Unless noted all tolerances are ± 1/64. Angles ±3°

RLT.COM, Inc.

PART NO. TK-7

Material:

DWG APRV:

DWG NO. Table Top Treb

REV A

DWG BY: RRG

SCALE NONE

SHEET

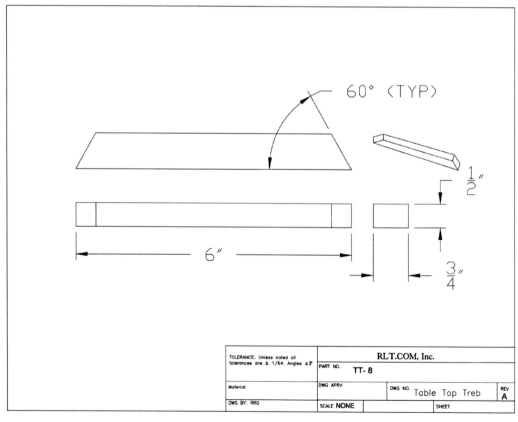

60° (TYP)

1½"

6"

¾"

TOLERANCE: Unless noted all tolerances are ± 1/64. Angles ±3°

RLT.COM, Inc.

PART NO. TT-8

Material:

DWG APRV:

DWG NO. Table Top Treb

REV A

DWG BY: RRG

SCALE NONE

SHEET

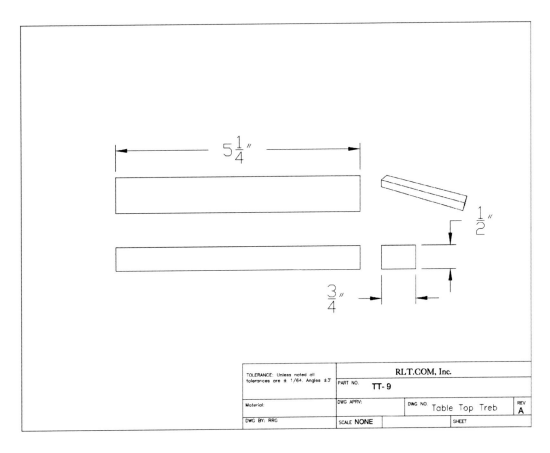

$5\frac{1}{4}''$

$\frac{1}{2}''$

$\frac{3}{4}''$

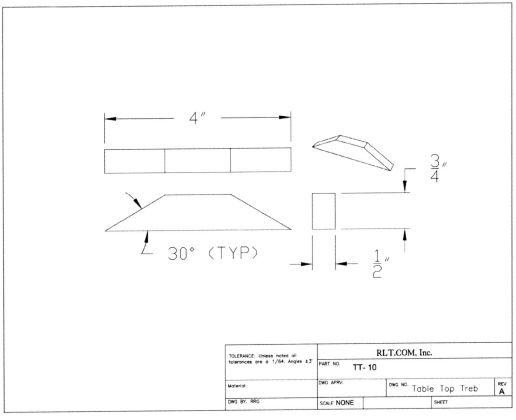

$4''$

$\frac{3}{4}''$

$30°$ (TYP)

$\frac{1}{2}''$

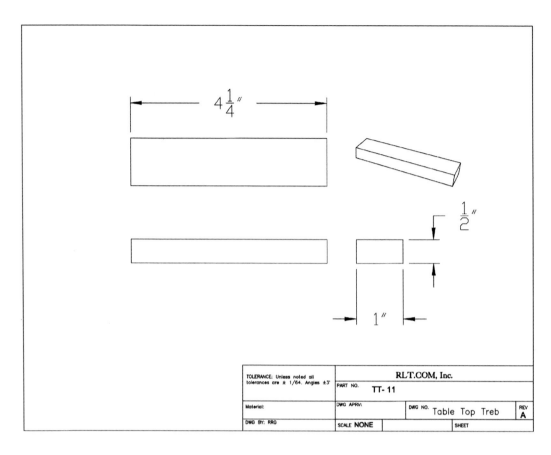

4 1/4″

1/2″

1″

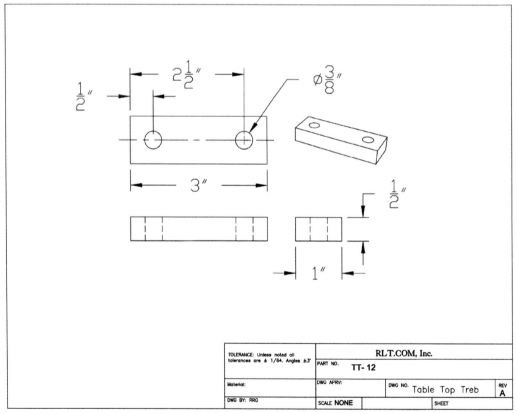

1/2″ 2 1/2″ Ø 3/8″

3″

1/2″

1″

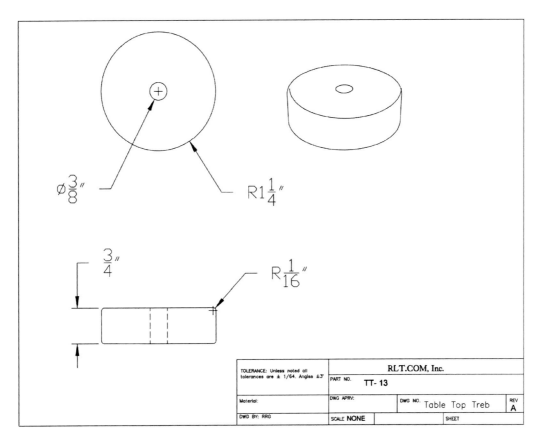

$\varnothing\frac{3}{8}''$

$R1\frac{1}{4}''$

$\frac{3}{4}''$

$R\frac{1}{16}''$

TOLERANCE: Unless noted all tolerances are ± 1/64. Angles ±3°	RLT.COM, Inc.		
	PART NO. TT- 13		
Material:	DWG APRV:	DWG NO. Table Top Treb	REV A
DWG BY: RRG	SCALE NONE	SHEET	

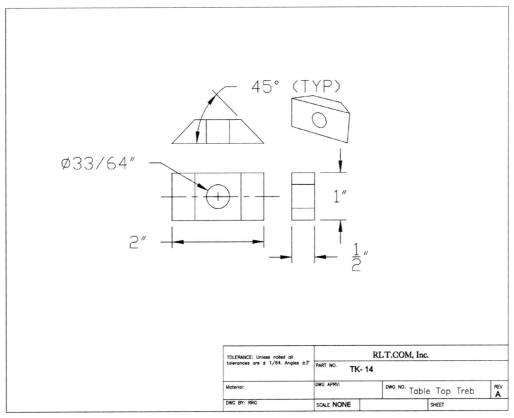

45° (TYP)

$\varnothing 33/64''$

$2''$

$1''$

$\frac{1}{2}''$

TOLERANCE: Unless noted all tolerances are ± 1/64. Angles ±3°	RLT.COM, Inc.		
	PART NO. TK- 14		
Material:	DWG APRV:	DWG NO. Table Top Treb	REV A
DWG BY: RRG	SCALE NONE	SHEET	

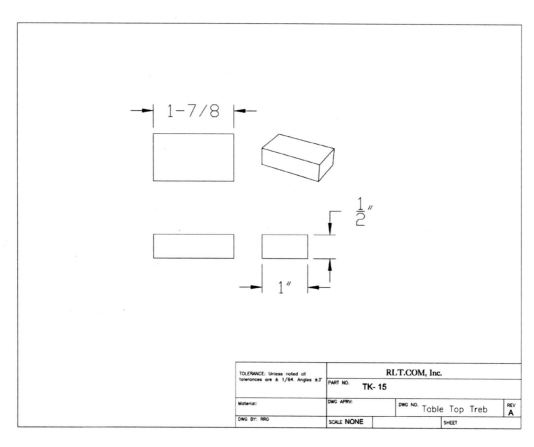

1-7/8

$\frac{1}{2}''$

1"

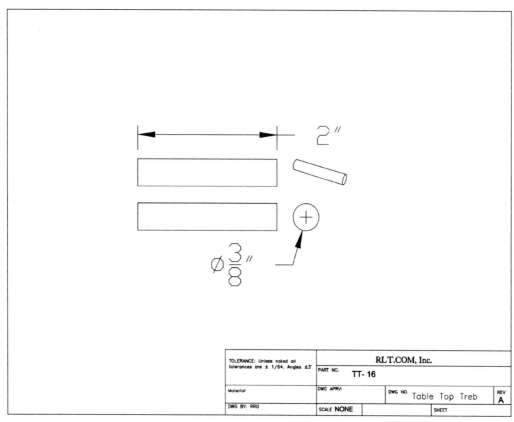

2"

$\phi\frac{3}{8}''$

Parts:

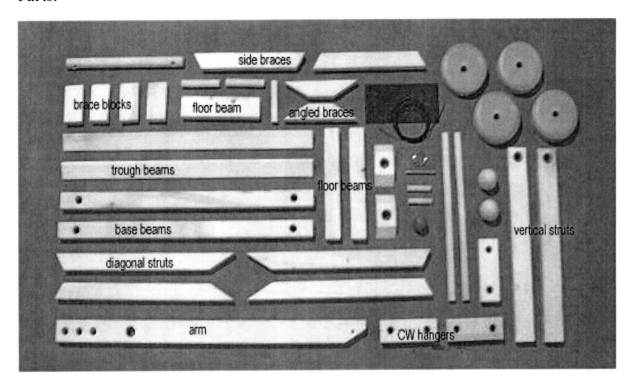

Building the frame:

Start with the vertical struts and the 4 ¼" floor beam. Glue the vertical beams to the ends of the floor beam so that add edges are flush and the side beams are parallel. Let the glue dry for at least an hour before removing the clamps.

Glue the four brace blocks as in Fig. 3 so that all edges are flush and the vertical struts are square (90 degrees) with the floor beam.

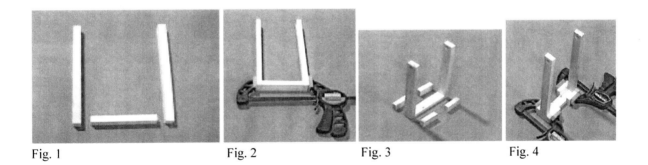

Fig. 1   Fig. 2   Fig. 3   Fig. 4

Make a mark in the center of the base beams, and a mark near the bottom of the vertical struts in the middle of the beam. Line up the marks so that the side beams are centered on the struts <u>with the wheel axle holes towards the bottom</u> (if your axle holes are centered, then this won't matter), and glue the side beams to the struts so that the bottoms are flush and the struts are square with the base beam (Fig. 6, next page).

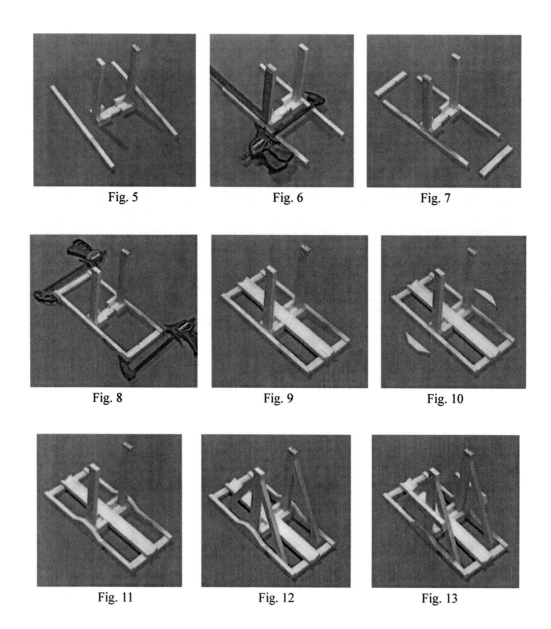

Fig. 5 Fig. 6 Fig. 7

Fig. 8 Fig. 9 Fig. 10

Fig. 11 Fig. 12 Fig. 13

Lay the 5 ¼" floor beams flat on either end of the base beams (Fig. 7). Slide them inside the base beams so that they are flush with the bottom and the ends of the side beams, but not the tops. Glue them in place and clamp (Fig. 8)

Glue the trough beams to the floor beams so that they form a V shaped trough in the middle. The trough should lay flat on all three of the floor beams.

Glue the angled braces to the outside of the vertical struts and to the top of the base beams as in Fig. 11.

Glue the diagonal struts to the vertical struts and base beams as in Fig. 12,
then the side beams as in fig. 13.

Building the arm:

Glue the arm reinforcing pieces to the sides of the arm so that the holes all line up.

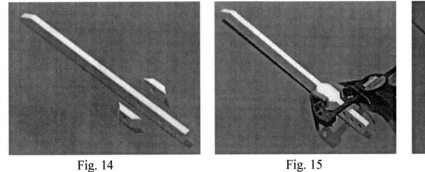

Fig. 14   Fig. 15   Fig. 16

Put some glue into the hole in the end of the arm, and insert the metal pin (file off any rough edges). Then install the arm onto the frame with the axle dowel. (On recent versions of the kit, the pin hole is angled for a better release point when firing) Secure the axle with the two small dowel pins in either end.

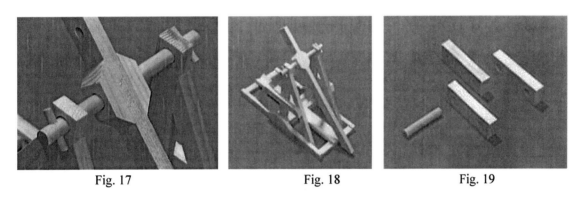

Fig. 17   Fig. 18   Fig. 19

The beveled edge of the arm is its bottom. The completed frame and arm assembly should look like fig. 18.:

Assemble the counterweight hanger like this: (No glue required)

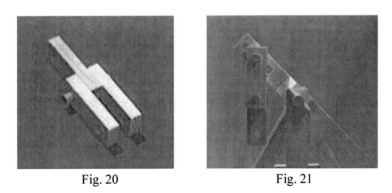

Fig. 20   Fig. 21

The counterweight hanger mounts to the center hole on the end of the arm. It will not work properly if installed in either of the other two holes, and may damage your machine.

The sling:

Poke 4 holes in each end of the pouch material about ½" from the end, like this:

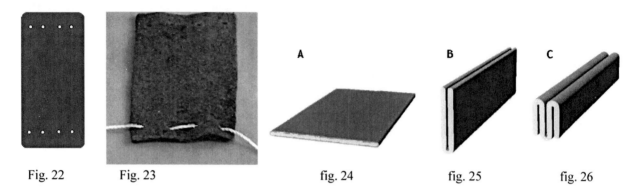

Fig. 22   Fig. 23   fig. 24   fig. 25   fig. 26

Thread a string through the holes (fig. 23) and fold the leather into an M shape (figs. 24, 25, 26) and pull the string tight through the holes. Then wrap the string once around the bottom of the M, back up to the top and tie it securely at the top of the M. Use a good square knot and fuse the ends (fig 31).

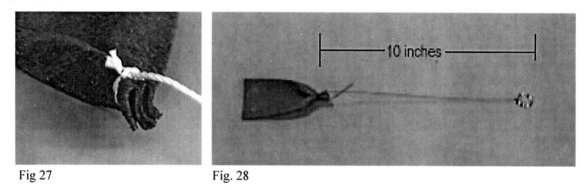

Fig 27   Fig. 28

On one end of the sling-pouch, cut the string about 14 inches long and tie it to the steel ring so that it is 10 inches from the knot at the pouch to the outer edge of the ring.
Your completed pouch should look like this:

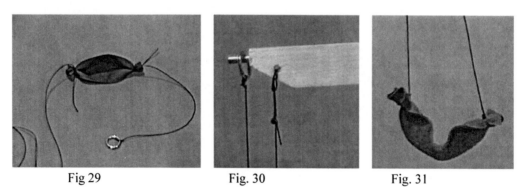

Fig 29   Fig. 30   Fig. 31

Tie the remaining end of the string through the hole in the end of the arm so that both sides of the sling are the same length. (Fig. 30, 31)

Counterweight Attachments:

There are two ways to attach the counterweights. Some historians and physics students believe that the best way to attach the counterweights is to hang them from the end of the arm. To do this, slip the weights onto the counterweight hanger and slide the counterweight pin in its hole to secure the weights in place.

Fig. 32

Fig. 33

Other historians and physics students think that the machine is more efficient when the counterweight is attached to the end of the arm. This can also make the machine unstable though, so add the wheels to the base (just insert the long dowels through the holes in the base and slip a wheel on the end of each one)

Remove the counterweight hanger, and insert the pin into the inner hole on the arm, slide the weights onto the arm and secure them with a pin in the outer hole.

Triggering:

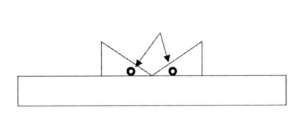

Fig. 33

Fig. 34

Using the three eye-screws and pin, Screw two of the eye-screws into the ends of the trough beams, indicated in the drawing above. Screw them in only about ½ inch, leaving the non-threaded part out of the wood.

WITH THE WHEELS OFF, Screw the third eye-screw into the bottom of the arm so that it lines up with the other two, and the pin can easily slide through all three as in figure 32. Be careful that you don't screw it in too far, and make sure the arm has enough clearance with the tabletop or floor. If the trigger holds the arm too close to the frame, you'll only be able to cock it with the wheels on.

Tuning:

A trebuchet can be a slightly complicated thing to tune properly. There are a lot of variables that all affect each other. Things that you can easily tune are:

The counterweight
The projectile weight
The sling length
The pin angle

The counterweight and the projectile:

Most people think that increasing the counterweight will make the machine throw farther. It might, a little. It might also make the trebuchet throw backwards or straight up, or you might just create more stress on the machine and break something. More counterweight usually only allows you to throw a comparably heavier projectile. Doubling your counterweight should mean that you can double the weight of your projectile and get the same performance. If the projectile is too light in relation to the tuning of the machine, it will probably come out of the sling at the wrong time.

More counterweight means that you have more power. To convert that power into more range, you'll need to adjust a few other things. Changing the counterweight without a corresponding change in the projectile weight will probably require a little additional tuning of the sling length. You'll see that the wooden missiles will need a different tuning than the iron missile. You'll have to decide which missile you want to tune for. This machine can send the wooden missiles about 25 feet, and the iron missile about 15 feet when tuned properly.

The sling length:

Watch the missile very carefully while firing the machine. If it flies in a high lob, the sling probably needs to be shorter. To make it shorter you can just tie knots in both sides of the sling. This is a great way to make fine adjustments in the sling length.

If the missile flies low to the ground and not very far, a longer sling should make it fly higher, and therefore farther.

The pin angle:

Once the sling length is right, watch the projectile as it is being fired. If it goes very high and not very far, the sling is releasing too early and the pin should be bent up, to a sharper angle. Tiny adjustments can make a big difference! If the projectile is going low, the pin needs to be moved down.

Once both sling length and pin angle are adjusted properly, the projectile should fly off the machine at about 45 degrees from horizontal. This is the optimum trajectory for the longest range.

The 21ˢᵗ Century Floating Arm Trebuchet PLANS!

We hope you enjoy building and shooting it as much as we've enjoyed creating it. So good luck, and have fun!

Parts List:

You will need: (see next page for details)

1 swatch of sling material	15 feet of twine	1 bolt 4 ½ inches long
1 spring clip (trigger)	6 large washers	1 eye-bolt 2" long and a wing-nut
4 square bend hook screws	1 bolt 5 ½ inches long	1 looped pin-hook
1 steel ring	20 wood screws	2 small washers
4 medium washers	2 large nuts (w/ nylon inserts)	2 small nuts
1 threaded steel rod	2 large nuts (plain)	3 plastic wheels

Wooden parts to cut: (see detail drawings following this page.)

1 base plate 21" x 7"	4 brace mounts 1" x 1" x 3" to tip.
2 trough plates 21 " x 1 ¾ " x 5/16"	2 rear track pieces 1" x 1" x 9" with a ¼" hole near one end
2 front track pieces 1" x 1" x 9"	4 counterweight guide post braces 16 ½" tip to tip
2 frame braces 1" x 1" x 3 1/8"	6 counterweight guide slot spacers 5/8" x ¾" x 1"
1 arm piece 1" x 1" x 36"	8 legs 1" x 1" x 11"
1 trigger piece ½" x ¾" x 5 ½"	4 vertical counterweight guides ¾" x ¾" x 39"
1 trigger other piece ½" x ¾" x 6 ½"	1 arm trigger rest
4 arm guides, 1" x 1" x 4" (to tip) with a hole	1 arm reinforcing piece ½" x 1" x 6 ½" (no holes)

Tools you will need to cut wood (this is what we use):
1. Table saw
2. Planer to smooth the wood and dimension it to the proper thickness
3. Miter saw, or chop saw.
4. Drill press

Tools you will need for assembly:
5. A Phillips-head screwdriver (#2 size will work for all screws)
6. Pliers or vice-grips
7. Two clamps capable of spanning 3" (Craftsman's mini bar clamps work great)
8. A carpenter's square, or any good 90 degree reference.
9. A crescent wrench or wrenches to fit the various nuts (7/16 and 9/16)
10. Scissors
11. Wood glue (or Elmer's white glue)

Hardware: You'll be able to get most of this stuff from any hardware store. Other things you might be able to find around the house. All of this hardware can also be found on-line

1 swatch of sling material – can be anything that's flexible and non-stretchy. Like denim, suede or soft leather (pig or goat leather works well) or plastic sheeting- especially the kind used for shade cloth. You'll need a finished size of 2.5" x 6" for your sling.

15 feet of twine – nylon mason's twine or hemp twine work best. Kite string is also fine.

1 bolt 4 ½ inches long – measurement does not include the bolt head (measure from under the head) ¼" diameter. Be sure the threads match the threads on the nuts you get. To be safe get size ¼ - 20   (twenty threads per inch)

1 spring clip (trigger) – You'll have to make this out of stiff but springy wire. Coat hanger wire works ok, but a good spring steel wire is better. Or you can use a clip of your own design. It has to span 1.5 inches.   (a broom handle clip will also work)

 (See fig. 20)

6 large washers – fender washers, ½" size hole, 1.5 inch diameter to the outside edge.

1 eye-bolt 2" long and a wing-nut – The eye bolt should be 2 inches long, not including the eye part. The eye should be ¼" diameter (inside) and the thickness of the bolt should be 3/16", or size 10-24 (10 gauge wire, 24 threads per inch). The wing nut will fit onto this bolt, so be sure it's the same size.

4 square bend hook screws – also known as an L-hook. it's a screw that has a 90 degree bend in it and no head.

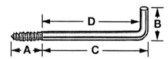   A = 5/8", B = ½", C = 1"

1 bolt 5 ½ inches long - measured not including the head (from tip to under the head) ¼" diameter, or size ¼ - 20.

1 looped pin-hook – you'll probably have to make this one yourself. It's basically an eye-bolt, but without any threads. You can make one out of coat hanger wire, the same size as the eye-bolt above, but with no threads.

1 steel ring – ½" inside diameter.   We DO NOT recommend using split key rings. These rings are made of brittle metal, and I've seen them shatter under load. This ring can experience loads up to 50 pound.

20 wood screws, #6 size works best, 1-5/8" long.
2 small washers – for the eye-screw. 3/6" inside diameter.
4 medium washers – for the ¼" bolts. ¼" standard washers are fine.
2 large nuts (w/ nylon inserts) size ½-13 The nylon inserts are also called nylock. It keeps them from jiggling loose.
2 large nuts (plain) also size ½-13. No nylon inserts, for easier installation.
2 small nuts ¼-20, to fit on the ¼" bolts. Nylock is a good idea for these too.
1 threaded steel rod – size ½"-13 (one half inch thick, thirteen threads per inch) the rod should be 14 inches long.
   (This is also known as "all-thread." It's usually available in 3-foot lengths that can be cut to size).
3 plastic wheels – 3 inch diameter, 7/8" width, ¼" plain bore.

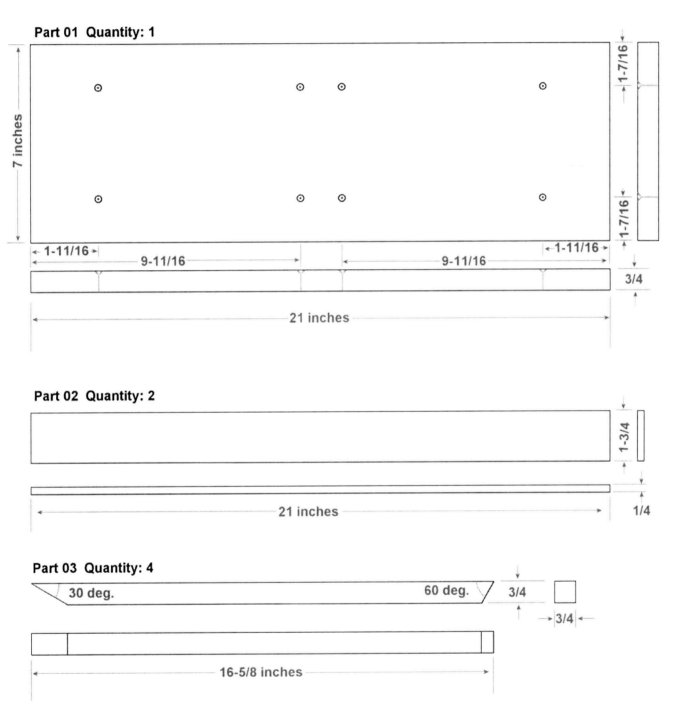

Part 01 Quantity: 1

7 inches

1-7/16

1-7/16

1-11/16   9-11/16   9-11/16   1-11/16

3/4

21 inches

Part 02 Quantity: 2

1-3/4

21 inches

1/4

Part 03 Quantity: 4

30 deg.   60 deg.   3/4

3/4

16-5/8 inches

32

Part 04 Quantity: 2

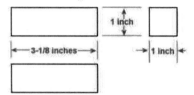

Part 05 Quantity: 4

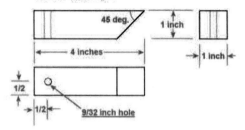

Part 06 Quantity: 4

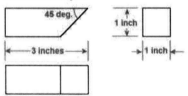

Part 07 Quantity: 1

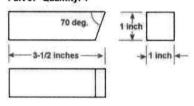

Part 08 Quantity: 1

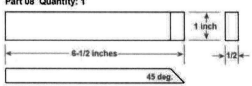

Part 09 Quantity: 1

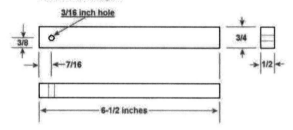

Part 10 Quantity: 1

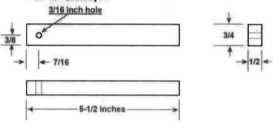

Part 11 Quantity: 6

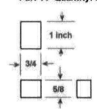

Part 12 Quantity: 1

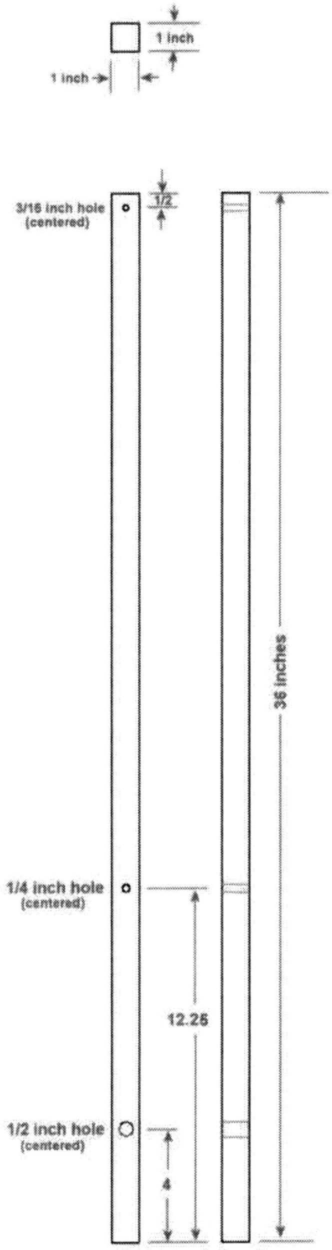

1 inch

1 inch →

3/16 inch hole
(centered)

1/2

36 inches

1/4 inch hole
(centered)

12.25

1/2 inch hole
(centered)

4

Part 13 Quantity: 4

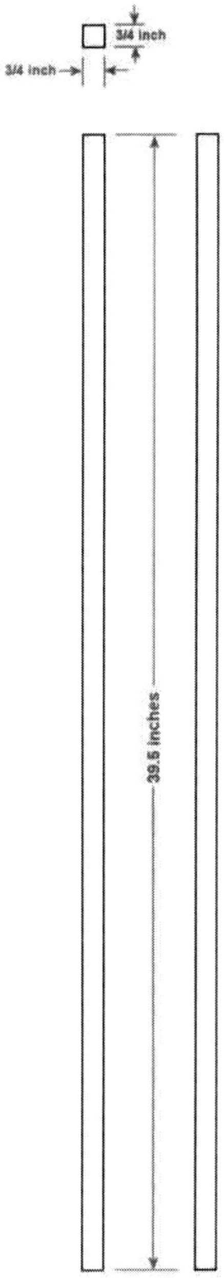

3/4 inch

3/4 inch →

39.5 inches

Part 14, quantity: 2

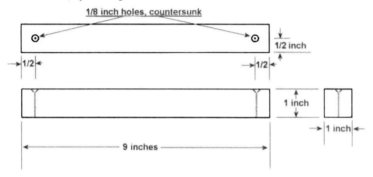

1/8 inch holes, countersunk

1/2 inch

1/2

1/2

1 inch

1 inch

9 inches

Part 15, quantity: 2

(all dimensions same as above, except as noted.)

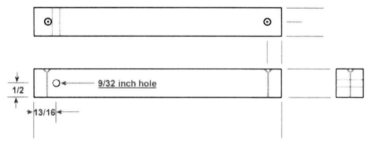

9/32 inch hole

1/2

13/16

Part 16, quantity: 8

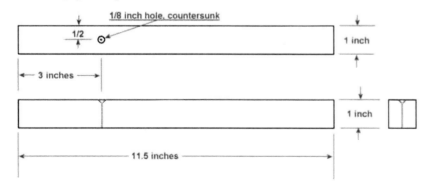

1/8 inch hole, countersunk

1/2

1 inch

3 inches

1 inch

11.5 inches

Assembly Instructions:
For updates and corrections to these instructions, please go to http://www.trebuchet.com/kit/updates

1. The Frame.

Start with the base plate. It has 8 holes pre-drilled in it for the leg screws. Use 8 of the black screws and screw them into the board until the tips just barely stick out of the top face of the board.

Using a straight-edge, draw an X on the bottom of each leg from corner to corner (Fig. 0) to locate the center. Put the screw-tip on one of the base screws in the center of the X and drive it in until the leg is tight against the base plate. Four of the legs have holes in the side of them. These legs go on the ends of the machine, two in front and two in the back. Be sure that the pre-drilled screw hole on the *side* of the leg is away from the base and is facing towards the side of the frame. (See Fig. 1) These holes will be used to attach the cross braces (See fig. 2).

Fig. 0

Fig. 1

It is important that the legs be perpendicular (90 degrees) to the base in all directions! We've tried to cut the ends as accurately as possible, but be sure to check anyway. If the end of the leg is not 90 degrees to the base, you can use strips of paper to shim the short side and make it perpendicular. Drive the screw into the base and the leg (making sure that the leg is 90 degrees from the base in all directions and that the screw-hole on the side of the leg is facing towards the side of the base). Be sure to drive the screw all the way in so that it is flush with the surface of the wood on the bottom of the frame. Do not over-tighten as that may strip out the screw from the wood.

Repeat this with all eight of the legs. IMPORTANT- be sure to leave a 5/8 inch gap between the center legs (Fig. 2b). On some kits, the pre-drilled holes in the base may be 1/8 inch off center. You may need to drive the screw a little off-center into the leg to make the gap exactly 5/8 inch (as in Fig. 2a). Use a counterweight guide spacer (the 1" x ¾" x 5/8" blocks) to make sure the gap is correct. There should be 3 1/8" space between the inside of the legs, and 7" of space between the middle and the front/rear legs (fig 2b).

Attach the two 3 1/8" braces, one on each end of the frame using the black screws (there is no brace for the center legs, they'll be braced a different way later). Make sure that all intersections are square! (90 degrees).

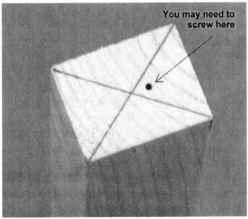
Fig. 2a

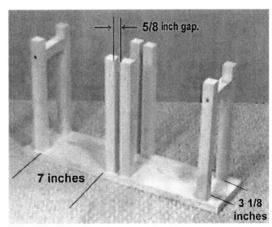
Fig. 2b

Get the two rear track pieces. These are the two 9" pieces with the ¼" hole near one end. Use the black screws to attach the track to the top of the legs so that the ¼" holes line up with each other (you should be able to put a long bolt through both of them). The holes should be near the back of the frame. Be sure all the connections are at 90 degrees and the screw heads are flush with the surface of the wood. The holes are countersunk on one side to allow for the screw heads. (Fig. 3)

Fig. 3

Attach the other two track pieces to the other four legs at the front of the frame. Make sure that the tracks are straight!

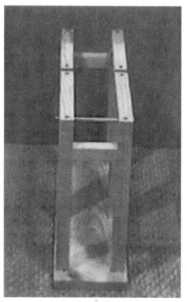

Fig. 4

Get two of the 1" x 1" x 3 ¾" arm-guide pieces (with a ¼" hole and one end cut 45 degrees) and place the short face against the inside edge of the track piece so that all the holes line-up. You may want to put a long bolt through all four pieces to insure that the alignment is good. The pointed ends of the guides should extend past the back end of the tracks and be angled up from the horizontal 10 or 15 degrees. These guides will keep the arm centered during firing. (See Fig. 5)

Install the plastic wheel with hubs on both sides (see fig. 6). Secure with the long bolt and a nut. Do not over tighten the nut since the wheel should spin freely on the bolt. Now glue the arm-guides to the inside of the track pieces and clamp them until the glue is set

Fig. 5

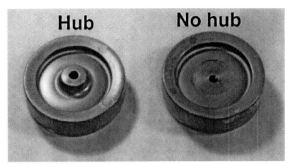

Fig. 6.

Now glue the 2 guide plates (21" x 1 ¾" x ¼"") to the insides of the legs of the frame to make a trough for the projectile to slide through (See Fig. 7).

Fig. 7

You now have a completed frame. Be sure that all the pieces are straight and solidly attached.

2. The Counterweight guides.

Start with the long (39") guide posts and spacer blocks (fig. 8). Glue the spacers flush to the top and bottom of the posts. If any of the posts is warped a little, glue them together so they bow away from each other in the middle. We can correct for the bowing later. (Fig. 9) .

Fig. 8

Fig. 9.

Glue is used for stronger joining. (The legs used screws instead of glue for easier alignment.) When gluing, be sure to put a thin layer of glue on the entire surface and clamp the pieces in place while the glue dries. Done properly, these glue joints are stronger than the wood itself.

Now that the guide slots are assembled, we can glue them to the base.

Once the guide channels are dry, clamp them to the base so they are flush with the inside edges of the center legs.(Fig. 10) When both sides are attached, make sure the threaded rod can slide easily all the way up and down the channels (Fig. 11).

Fig. 10

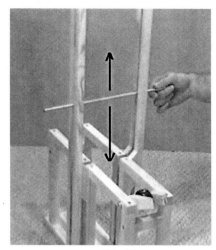

Fig 11

(Note: ignore the standoffs in fig. 11. They are from an older version of the model.)
If they are not straight, while the glue is still wet adjust the clamps and the guides until they are as straight as you can get them. It's important that the threaded rod can slide easily between the guides and the legs.

Glue the counterweight guide brace mounts to the side of the rear and front legs as in Fig. 12. The tops of the mounts should be at the same height at the top of the frame piece between the legs. Once this glue has dried, glue the guide braces in place. The guide braces can be used to "push-in" the guide post if it is bowed out. Be sure to glue it and clamp it well in all three points of contact! (fig. 13)

Fig 12.

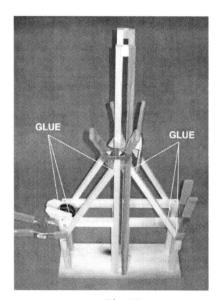

Fig. 13

3. The Arm

Start with the 1" x 1" x 34" piece. The two remaining arm guides should be glued to the arm so that they point to the bottom of the arm and the holes are lined up with the same sized hole in the arm. Using the short bolt, attach the wheels to the arm guides so that the flat side is against the arm assembly, and the bolt head and nut can fit inside the counter-bored side. Put the thin nut on this bolt, and tighten just enough so that the wheels can spin freely. See fig. 14.

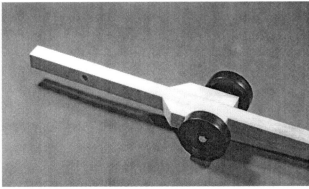

Fig. 14.

Fig. 15

Glue the arm reinforcing piece on the top of the arm, and the trigger rest block on the bottom of the arm and flush with the bottom of the arm, as in Fig. 15.

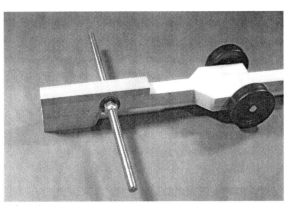

Fig 16

Fig. 17   (not to scale)

Get the long threaded rod and insert it through the big hole near the end of the arm. The rod should be centered on the arm as exactly as you can get it. Put a plain nut on each end of the rod and tighten against the sides of the arm.
When you are done, make sure that the arm is centered on the rod. Your arm should look like Fig 16 now.

Next, put the long eye-bolt (with a medium washer) in the hole on the side of the arm. Put a friction washer on the other side, then the pin hook loop and the other friction washer, then finally the wing-nut. The small black washers are friction washers. By adjusting the angle of the pin, you'll be able to fine-tune the machine.

Install the arm onto the frame by turning it sideways (so the threaded rod is vertical) and rotate it so that the threaded rod slides between the counterweight channels. The trigger rest block should be on the bottom of the arm when the arm is horizontal and resting on all three wheels.

Now add a large washer and a nut to either side of the threaded rod, making sure that it is centered on the frame. It is very important that it be centered so that the arm doesn't hit any part of the frame when the counterweights pull the threaded rod down. The washers should slide loosely against the vertical guides! Don't tighten the nuts against the guides! Any resistance will only degrade the performance of the trebuchet.

4. The Trigger.

The trigger is a simple trap-door mechanism. Lift the arm's trigger rest block up to the top of the counterweight channels. The short trigger piece (with one small hole in it) will be the platform that the arm rests on. Attach it using the square hook screw to the counterweight guide as in fig. 18. Next, attach the other trigger piece under the short one, as in fig. 19.

Fig. 18

Fig. 19

Make a loop in the piece of wire. You can use a pair of pliers to wrap it around a nail, or make a wire jig by driving two nails into a board about ¼" apart, then cut the heads off the nails. You can also get a wire bending jig from most well-stocked hardware and tool shops. We got this one from Mcmaster Carr (www.Mcmaster.com). Then bend the ends to form a spring-clip shape, as in fig. 20. The clip should be 1.5 inches between the ends and ¾ inches deep.
.

NOTE: We've replaced the wire with a pre-formed spring clip in this kit, but we didn't have time to update the photos!

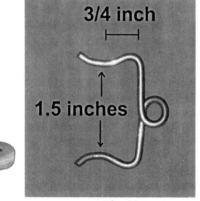

A wire bending tool   Fig. 20

Fig 21.

The spring clip will hold the trap door closed (fig 21) Tie a string onto the loop. To fire the machine simply jerk the spring clip off of the trap doors, but be sure to stay a safe distance off to the side of the machine!

Make sure the trap door pieces can swing easily and freely. You may need to lubricate them or make the hole a little bigger if necessary to make them swing easily. Use the other two hook screws to catch the trap doors when they flip open. If there is nothing to catch them, they can swing around and strike the arm during firing. This will damage your machine! The hook placement is shown in Fig. 22.

To make a safety for the trigger, drive the small silver screw into the hole on the free end of the long trigger piece. Leave about ½" of the screw sticking out of the wood. Then tie a loop of string around this screw and to the hook directly above it (Fig. 21). When you are ready to fire the machine, be sure to remove the loop of string first.

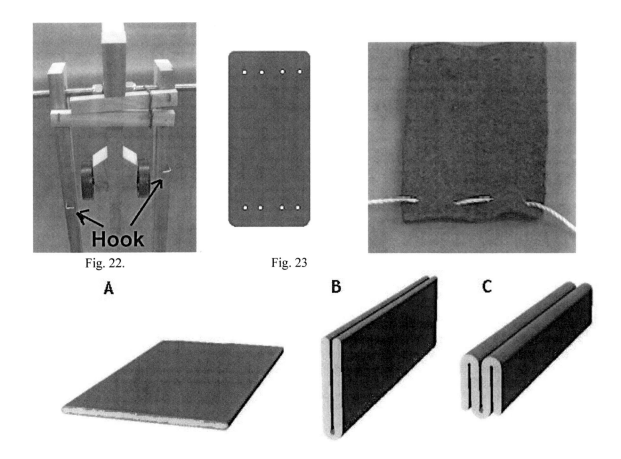

Fig. 22.　　　　　　Fig. 23

Hook

A　　　　　B　　　　　C

5. The Sling.

Get the sling pouch material and lay it flat. Punch holes in it according to fig. 23. Fold the edges of this strip (lengthwise) up (**B**), then in half back down (**C**) to form an 'M' shape. Turn this over so the 'M' is now a 'W' (**D**).

Tie each end tight with the twine about ¾" from each end of the sling pouch so that the knot is on the top of the 'W', then push the center of the 'W' inside out (through the bottom) and you should be left with a perfect sling-pouch.

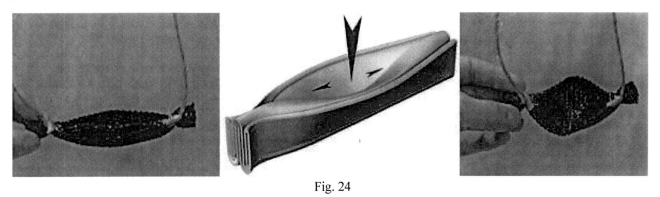

Fig. 24

Now cut the twine 26" from each end of the sling. On one end tie the steel ring, and tie the other end to the eye-screw on the arm. Place the wooden ball in the pouch and the steel ring over the pin. Make sure that the sling-pouch hangs properly and cradles the ball so that it won't easily slip out. If one side of the sling is too long, you can just tie a knot in the string to make it shorter. This also gives you the opportunity to lengthen the sling if needed by simply untying the knot!

6. The Counterweights

There are many things around the house you can use for counterweights. The simplest solution is to use an old pair of socks and fill them with nuts and bolts, or pennies, or even small rocks until you get the weight you need. We did our tests using $10 worth of pennies as the counterweight. Here are some weights:

Pennies: 350 ($3.50 worth) = 2 lbs.
½" hex nuts: 50 (one box) = 3 lbs.
Water: 1 quart = 2 lbs.
Sand: 1 quart = 3 ½ lbs. (approximate)

You need to have the same mount of weight on each side of the machine. It's ok if one side is *slightly* heavier than the other, but it's not the best thing to do.

You can fill the optional welded steel boxes (available at Trebuchet.com) with 500 pennies each (totaling $10 worth) for 9 lbs. of counterweight. Enough to toss a golf ball well over 100 feet (we got 180 feet after some tuning!) Or fill them with sand, fishing weights, tire balancing weights, or lead shot from a sporting goods store for more weight and even more distance.

Once you've got an appropriate weight material, put an equal amount on each side, attached loosely onto the threaded rod. Start with only about 5 lbs. Total (2 ½ lbs. per side) until you get used to how the machine works. With 5 lbs you should be able to fling a golf ball about 50-75 feet. It may take some tuning initially to achieve this result.
DO NOT EVER use more than 15 lbs total (including the weight of the boxes). The machine is not designed for this much weight. You should be able to achieve 200 feet with a golf ball and 10 lbs of counterweight (if tuned well). Also, do not fire the machine without a projectile in the pouch. This is a "dry fire" and may damage the machine.

7. Firing the machine.

Pick a spot that is flat and level to set the machine on. The release pin comes very close to the ground during firing, so be sure there is clearance for it. Pull the arm towards the back of the machine, then grab the threaded rod and pull it up until it hits the top of the guide channels. Carefully set the trigger and immediately move away from the machine. Never stand near the machine when it is cocked!

With the machine cocked and the safety loop on, pull the sling into the trough and load the wooden ball (or a golf ball) into the pouch so that the pouch goes over and under the ball, not around its sides. Put the steel ring over the release pin on the end of the arm, and re-tension the sling so that the ring doesn't fall off the pin. You are now cocked and loaded, so be especially careful!

Make sure there is nothing for 200 feet in front of or in back of the machine! A trebuchet that hasn't been tuned can just as easily throw something backwards, forwards, or even straight up. Perhaps you should wear a hardhat too!

With the machine aimed, carefully remove the safety and stand at least 6 feet away from the side of the trebuchet. Countdown so that everyone around knows what's about to happen, and jerk the trigger string to remove the hasp. Then watch it fly!

Always remember that the arm moves very fast. It can knock you out if it hits your head. And the pin on the end can act like a sharp hook swinging around. It could tear your skin or poke out your eyes if you stand too close when it goes off.

NEVER stand over, in front of or behind a cocked machine, whether it is loaded or not! ALWAYS use a safety device when loading the trebuchet, and never fire it at any person or thing. The trebuchet should only be fired into an open field and under adult supervision.

8. Tuning the machine.

A trebuchet is a slightly complicated thing to tune. There are a lot of variables that all affect each other. Things that you can easily tune are: The counterweight, The projectile weight, The sling length, The pin angle, and more.

The counterweight:
The first thing most people think is that increasing the counterweight will make the machine throw farther. It might, a little. It might also make the trebuchet throw backwards or straight up. More counterweight usually only allows you to throw a comparably heavier projectile. Doubling your counterweight should mean that you can double the weight of your

projectile and get the same performance. If the projectile is too light in relation to the tuning of the machine, it will probably come out of the sling at the wrong time.

More counterweight means that you have more power. To convert that power into more range, you'll need to adjust a few other things. Changing the counterweight without a corresponding change in the projectile weight will probably require a little additional tuning of the pin angle and/or sling length.

Note: Do not "dry-fire" the machine (firing with no projectile loaded) with more than 6 lbs. of counterweight. Also do not exceed 15 lbs. of total counterweight. Either of these can cause the threaded rod to bend and degrade the performance of the machine.

The sling length:
Watch the sling very carefully while firing the machine. If it never seems to quite catch up to the angle of the arm, it needs to be shorter. If it swings around too fast and gets ahead of the arm (or comes off the pin too early), the sling probably needs to be longer. Making it longer is tough, but to make it shorter you can just tie a knot in both sides of the sling. This is a great way to make fine adjustments in the sling length.

The pin angle:
Once the sling length is right, watch the projectile as it is being fired. If it goes very high and not very far, the sling is releasing too early and the pin should be moved up, to a sharper angle. Tiny adjustments can make a big difference! If the projectile is going low, the pin needs to be moved a little straighter.

Once both sling length and pin angle are adjusted properly, the projectile should fly off the machine at about 30 degrees from horizontal. This is the optimum trajectory for the longest range. Why not 45 degrees? This machine imparts a backspin on the ball, which will make it want to climb as it travels through the air. This is called the Magnus effect and is also how baseball pitchers throw curve balls by using sidespin.

How to calculate your range efficiency:
The range efficiency is a measure of how well your machine converts all the energy available to it into throwing the ball. It's really simple - the ball travels in an arc when it's thrown. There are two components to this arc, the vertical (how high it goes) and the horizontal (how far it goes). They relate to each other by the angle that the ball was thrown.

Using the physics of ballistic motion, and some trigonometry, we've derived this equation for the maximum theoretical range a machine like this can throw.

$$2 * (CW * drop) / P = \text{Theoretical range.}$$

CW is the weight, in ounces of your total counterweight. If you have 9 lbs, then that is 144 ounces. The **drop** is the number of inches it falls when firing. This kit drops 26 inches. So your available energy is 144 * 26 = 3744 inch-ounces of energy. Multiply by **2** to get 7488, and then divide by **P** (the weight of your projectile in ounces). If your projectile is 3 ounces, your maximum theoretical range is 7488 / 3 = 2496 inches, or 208 feet (2496 divided by 12 inches = 208 feet)

The theoretical range is never really possible though. Most machines are never more than about 50% efficient due to things like friction, air resistance, non-perfect release angles, compression and elasticity of the various parts, etc., so your maximum *realistic* range is about half (50%) of your maximum theoretical range. Or:

$$CW * drop / P = \text{realistic maximum range.}$$

Now that you know the realistic and theoretical range of your machine, you can calculate your efficiency! If you calculate your theoretical range with the CW and projectile weights you have, then measure the actual distance of your shot, your efficiency is

Actual measured range / Theoretical range * 100 = percent efficiency
Actual measured range / Realistic range * 100 = percent effectiveness

If you used 9 lbs of CW, and a 3 ounce ball, and threw it 90 feet, then your efficiency is 90 / 208 * 100 = 43% efficient. But the effectiveness of the machine is 86%. Not bad! But you'll have to do a LOT of tuning to get this kind of efficiency!

When we shot a 1 ½ ounce golf ball 202 feet, we were using 15 lbs of CW. What was our efficiency? How did we do compared to the maximum realistic range? How effective was that shot?

The best efficiencies happen when the counterweight is between 50 and 100 times as heavy as the projectile.

The Warwolf Trebuchet

We hope you enjoy building and shooting it as much as we've enjoyed creating it. So good luck, and have fun!

Hardware :

1 swatch of burlap 6" x 8"	30 5/16" dowels 2 ½" long	4 wood screws 1" long
15 feet of light rope (¼" or less)	4 3/16" dowels 1 1/4" long	20 small nails
1 dowel ½" x 2"	4 3/8" wood plugs (optional)	16 wood screws 1-5/8" long
5 steel rings,	1 welded steel ring,	1 trigger (We use the
3/4" inside diameter	(1" inside diameter)	Seadog 4" bronze pelican hook. Or, you can use anything that works as a quick release under tension.)

Wooden parts (see drawings):

2 base beams 34" long
4 base cross-braces 11 ¼" long
1 base cross beam 31-1/4" long
2 outrigger braces 21 ½ " long, tip-to-tip
2 side beams 14" long
4 A-frame legs, 32" long
2 vertical beams, 29 ½" long
1 plywood base plate
2 plywood bucket sides (12" x 6")
2 plywood bucket sides (6 sided)
2 CW bucket end plates 9" x 5"
1 CW bucket bottom plate 10 ½" x 5"

1 trough board 34" long
4 axle block mount plates 6 ½" long" with four holes
2 axle block plates 6 ½" long, grooved, with two holes
2 axle block plates 6 ½" long, grooved, with four holes
1 small block.
1 main axle dowel ¾" x 11 1/2"
1 counterweight axle dowel ¾" x 6 1/8"
1 main arm beam 35" long
2 short arm beams 23 ½" long with two big holes
2 arm plates 23 ½" long tip-to-tip
2 arm spacers 3 ¼" long tip-to-tip
2 counterweight hangers 15" x 2 3/8" with a big hole

Tools you will need:

1. A table saw
2. A drill press
3. A miter or chop saw
4. A Phillips-head screwdriver (#2 size will work for all screws)
5. Two or four clamps capable of spanning 6" (Craftsman's mini bar clamps work great)
6. A carpenter's square, or any good 90 degree reference.
7. Scissors
8. A light hammer

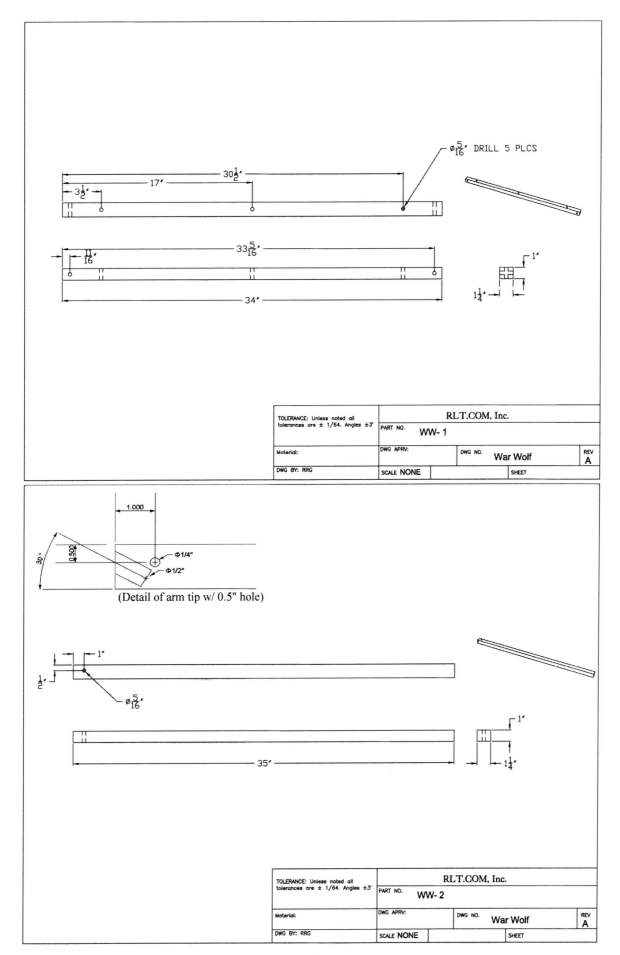

ø5/16" DRILL 5 PLCS

30 1/2"

17"

3 1/2"

33 5/16"

11/16"

34"

1"

1 1/4"

TOLERANCE: Unless noted all tolerances are ± 1/64. Angles ±3°

RLT.COM, Inc.

PART NO. WW- 1

Material:

DWG APRV:

DWG NO. War Wolf

REV A

DWG BY: RRG

SCALE NONE

SHEET

1.000

30°

Ø.500

Φ1/4"

Φ1/2"

(Detail of arm tip w/ 0.5" hole)

1"

1/2"

ø5/16"

35"

1"

1 1/4"

TOLERANCE: Unless noted all tolerances are ± 1/64. Angles ±3°

RLT.COM, Inc.

PART NO. WW- 2

Material:

DWG APRV:

DWG NO. War Wolf

REV A

DWG BY: RRG

SCALE NONE

SHEET

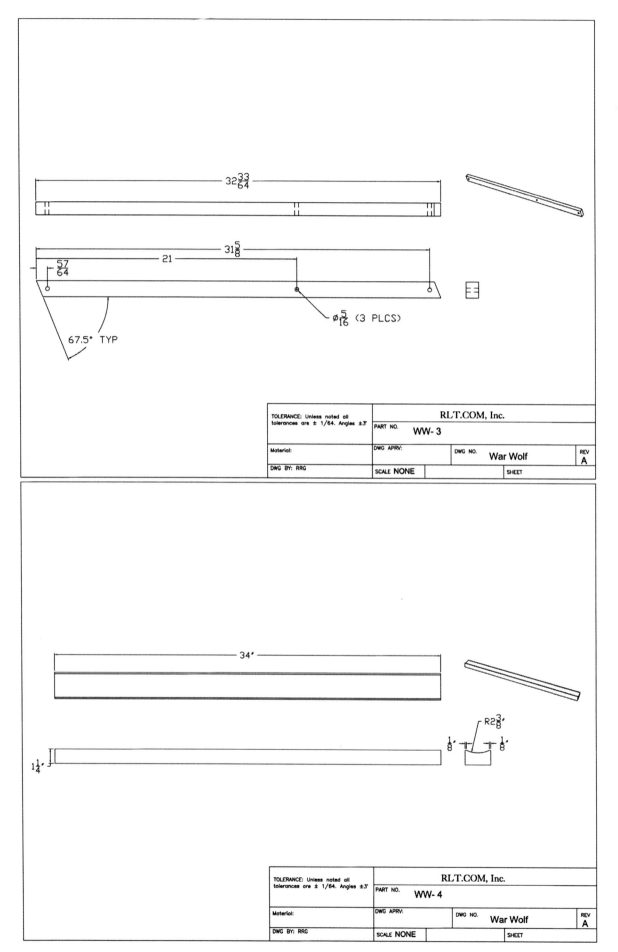

$32\frac{33}{64}$

$31\frac{5}{8}$

21

$\frac{57}{64}$

$\phi\frac{5}{32}$ (3 PLCS)

67.5° TYP

TOLERANCE: Unless noted all tolerances are ± 1/64. Angles ±3°	RLT.COM, Inc.		REV
	PART NO. WW-3		
Material:	DWG APRV:	DWG NO. War Wolf	A
DWG BY: RRG	SCALE NONE	SHEET	

34″

$R2\frac{3}{8}$″

$\frac{1}{8}$″ $\frac{1}{8}$″

$1\frac{1}{4}$″

TOLERANCE: Unless noted all tolerances are ± 1/64. Angles ±3°	RLT.COM, Inc.		REV
	PART NO. WW-4		
Material:	DWG APRV:	DWG NO. War Wolf	A
DWG BY: RRG	SCALE NONE	SHEET	

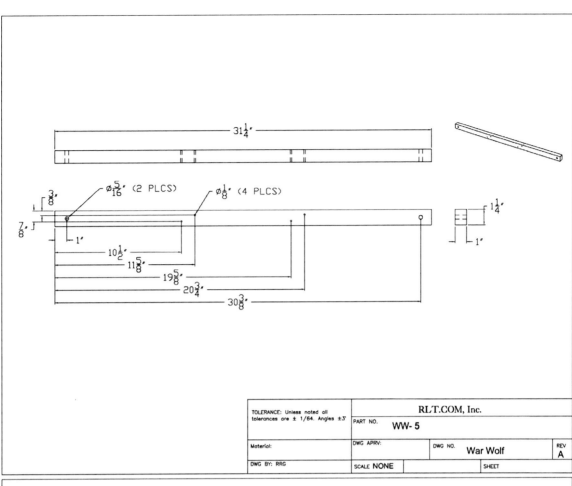

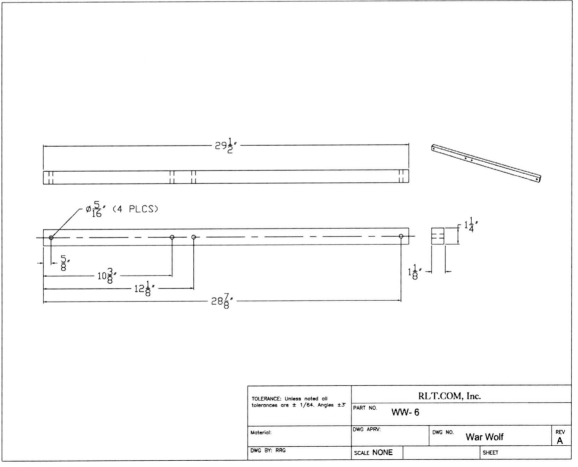

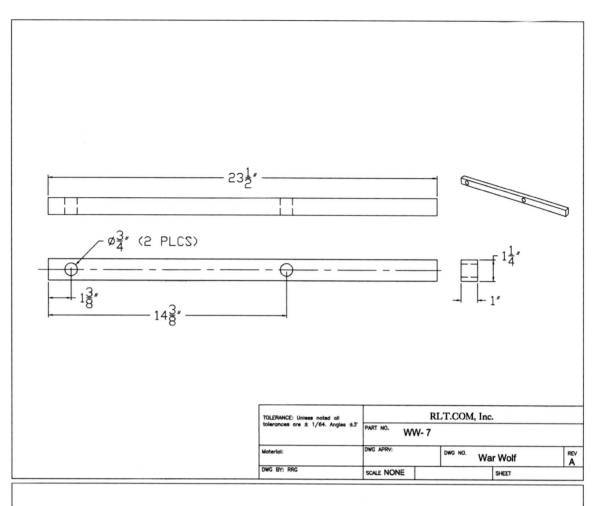

$\phi \frac{3}{4}''$ (2 PLCS)

$23\frac{1}{2}''$

$1\frac{3}{8}''$

$14\frac{3}{8}''$

$1\frac{1}{4}''$

$1''$

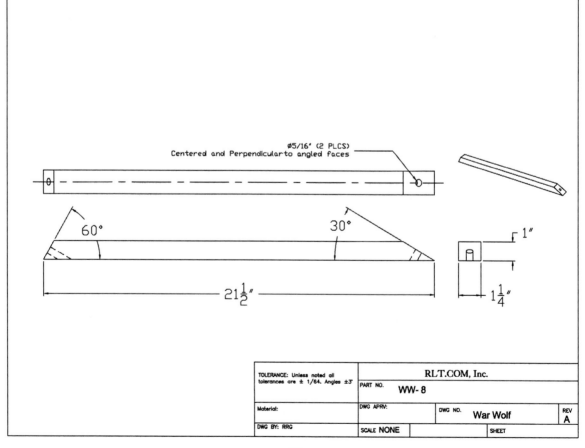

$\phi 5/16''$ (2 PLCS)
Centered and Perpendicular to angled faces

60°

30°

$21\frac{1}{2}''$

$1''$

$1\frac{1}{4}''$

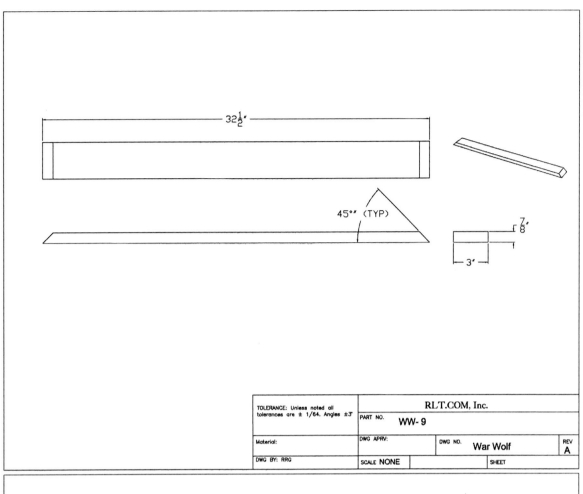

32½″

45°″ (TYP)

7/8″

3″

TOLERANCE: Unless noted all tolerances are ± 1/64. Angles ±3°

RLT.COM, Inc.

PART NO. WW-9

Material:

DWG APRV:

DWG NO. War Wolf

REV A

DWG BY: RRG

SCALE NONE

SHEET

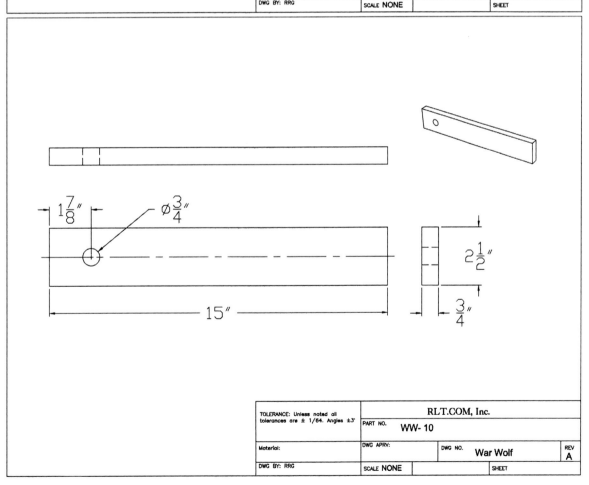

1 7/8″

ø 3/4″

15″

2 1/2″

3/4″

TOLERANCE: Unless noted all tolerances are ± 1/64. Angles ±3°

RLT.COM, Inc.

PART NO. WW-10

Material:

DWG APRV:

DWG NO. War Wolf

REV A

DWG BY: RRG

SCALE NONE

SHEET

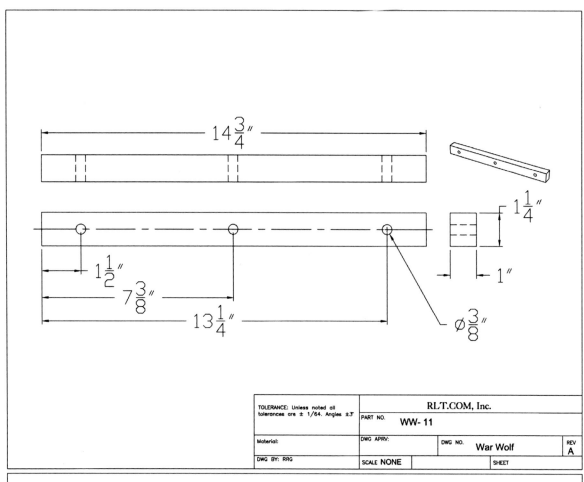

$14\frac{3}{4}''$

$1\frac{1}{4}''$

$1''$

$1\frac{1}{2}''$

$7\frac{3}{8}''$

$13\frac{1}{4}''$

$\varnothing\frac{3}{8}''$

TOLERANCE: Unless noted all tolerances are ± 1/64. Angles ±3°	RLT.COM, Inc.		
	PART NO. WW- 11		
Material:	DWG APRV:	DWG NO. War Wolf	REV A
DWG BY: RRG	SCALE NONE		SHEET

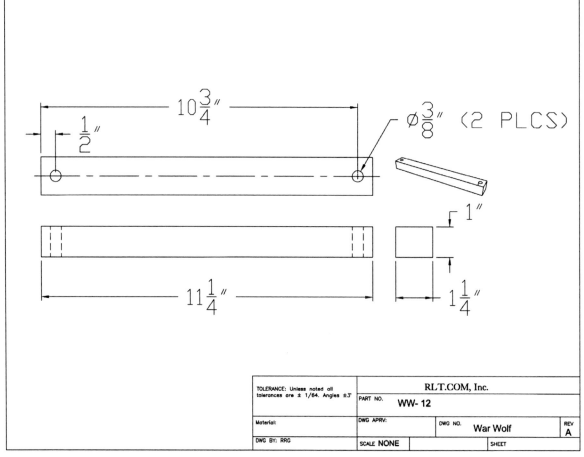

$10\frac{3}{4}''$

$\varnothing\frac{3}{8}''$ (2 PLCS)

$\frac{1}{2}''$

$1''$

$11\frac{1}{4}''$

$1\frac{1}{4}''$

TOLERANCE: Unless noted all tolerances are ± 1/64. Angles ±3°	RLT.COM, Inc.		
	PART NO. WW- 12		
Material:	DWG APRV:	DWG NO. War Wolf	REV A
DWG BY: RRG	SCALE NONE		SHEET

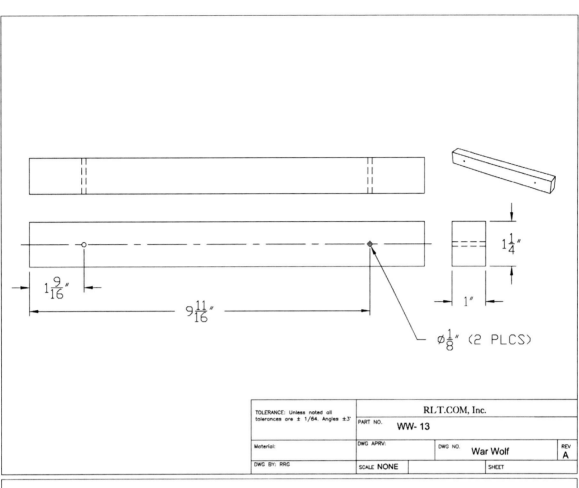

$1\frac{9}{16}''$

$9\frac{11}{16}''$

$1\frac{1}{4}''$

$1''$

$\phi\frac{1}{8}''$ (2 PLCS)

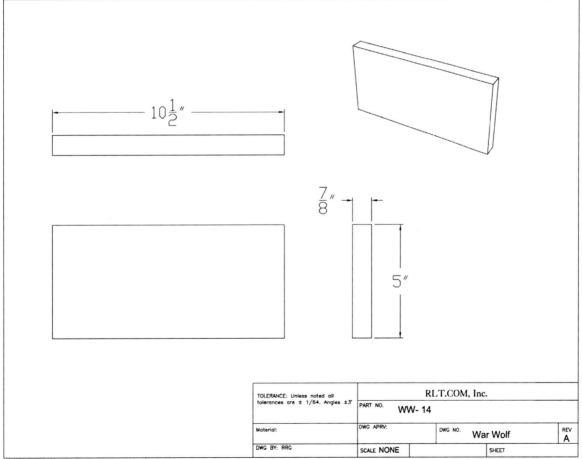

$10\frac{1}{2}''$

$\frac{7}{8}''$

$5''$

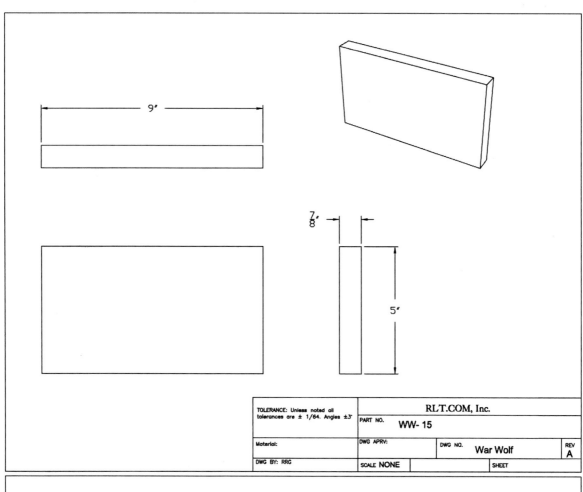

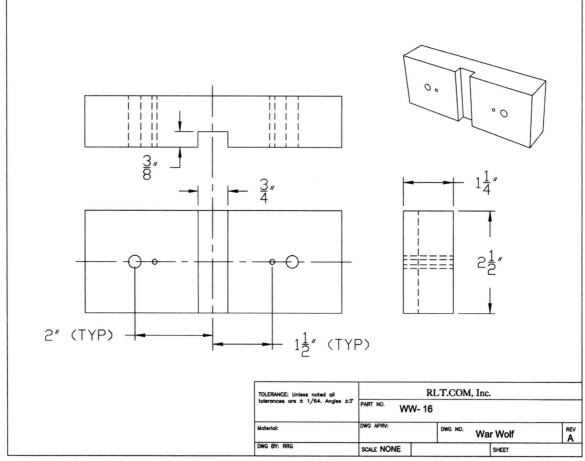

2" (TYP)

1½" (TYP)

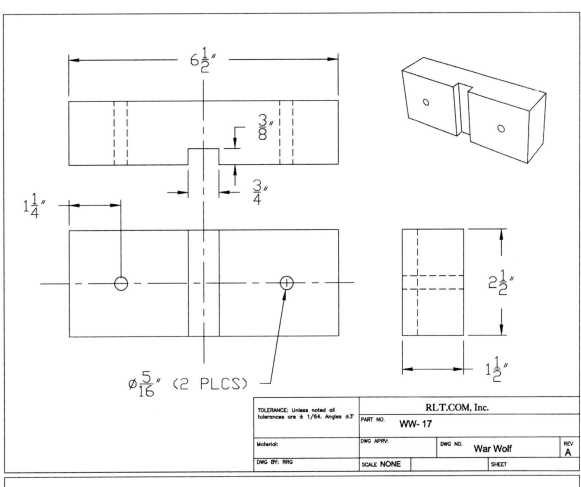

$6\frac{1}{2}''$

$\frac{3}{8}''$

$\frac{3}{4}''$

$1\frac{1}{4}''$

$\varnothing\frac{5}{16}''$ (2 PLCS)

$2\frac{1}{2}''$

$1\frac{1}{2}''$

TOLERANCE: Unless noted all tolerances are ± 1/64. Angles ±3°	RLT.COM, Inc.		
	PART NO. WW- 17		
Material:	DWG APRV:	DWG NO. War Wolf	REV A
DWG BY: RRG	SCALE NONE		SHEET

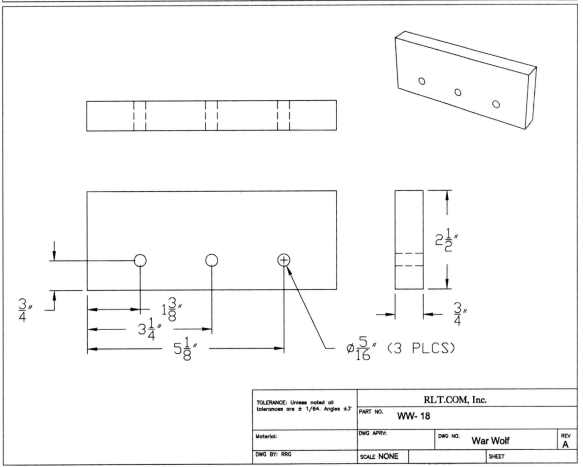

$2\frac{1}{2}''$

$\frac{3}{4}''$

$\frac{3}{4}''$

$1\frac{3}{8}''$

$3\frac{1}{4}''$

$5\frac{1}{8}''$

$\varnothing\frac{5}{16}''$ (3 PLCS)

TOLERANCE: Unless noted all tolerances are ± 1/64. Angles ±3°	RLT.COM, Inc.		
	PART NO. WW- 18		
Material:	DWG APRV:	DWG NO. War Wolf	REV A
DWG BY: RRG	SCALE NONE		SHEET

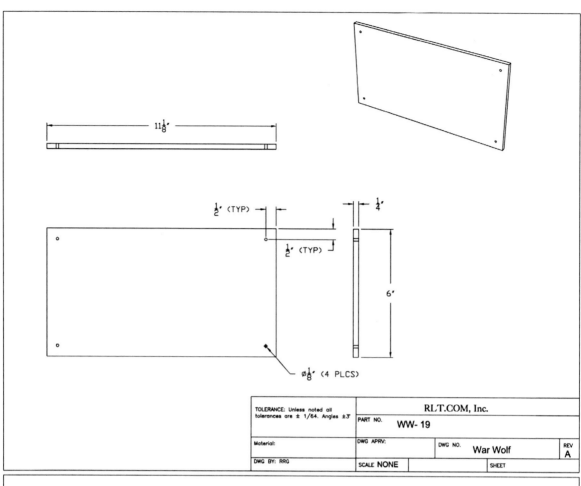

11⅛"

½" (TYP)   ¼"

½" (TYP)

6"

ø⅛" (4 PLCS)

TOLERANCE: Unless noted all tolerances are ± 1/64. Angles ±3°	RLT.COM, Inc.		
	PART NO. WW-19		
Material:	DWG APRV:	DWG NO. War Wolf	REV A
DWG BY: RRG	SCALE NONE	SHEET	

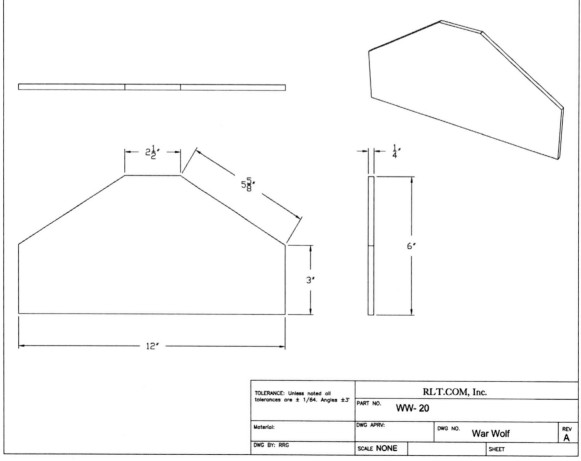

2½"

5⅝"

¼"

6"

3"

12"

TOLERANCE: Unless noted all tolerances are ± 1/64. Angles ±3°	RLT.COM, Inc.		
	PART NO. WW-20		
Material:	DWG APRV:	DWG NO. War Wolf	REV A
DWG BY: RRG	SCALE NONE	SHEET	

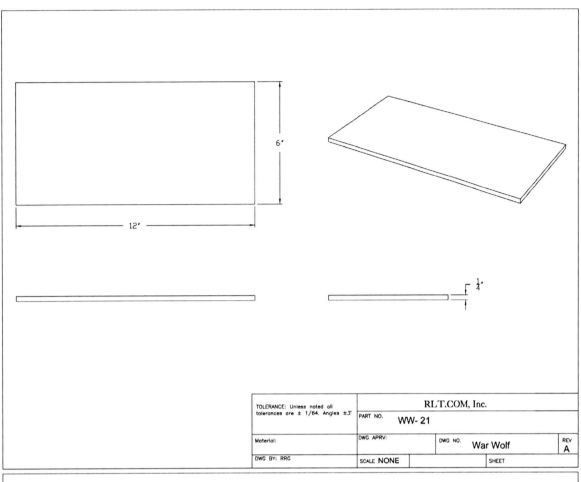

6″

12″

1/4″

TOLERANCE: Unless noted all tolerances are ± 1/64. Angles ±3°	RLT.COM, Inc.			
	PART NO. WW- 21			
Material:	DWG APRV:	DWG NO. War Wolf		REV A
DWG BY: RRG	SCALE NONE		SHEET	

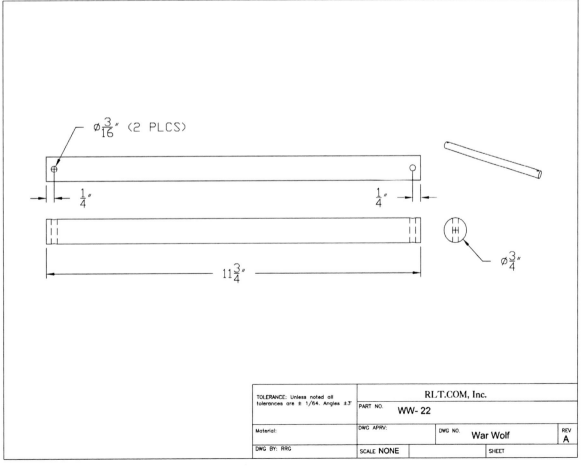

$\phi\frac{3}{16}''$ (2 PLCS)

$\frac{1}{4}''$

$\frac{1}{4}''$

$11\frac{3}{4}''$

$\phi\frac{3}{4}''$

TOLERANCE: Unless noted all tolerances are ± 1/64. Angles ±3°	RLT.COM, Inc.			
	PART NO. WW- 22			
Material:	DWG APRV:	DWG NO. War Wolf		REV A
DWG BY: RRG	SCALE NONE		SHEET	

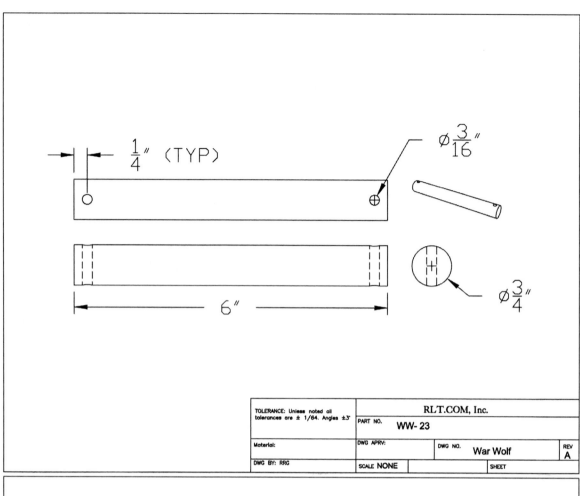

$\frac{1}{4}''$ (TYP)

$\phi\frac{3}{16}''$

6″

$\phi\frac{3}{4}''$

TOLERANCE: Unless noted all tolerances are ± 1/64. Angles ±3°	RLT.COM, Inc.
	PART NO. WW-23
Material:	DWG APRV: / DWG NO. War Wolf / REV A
DWG BY: RRG	SCALE NONE / SHEET

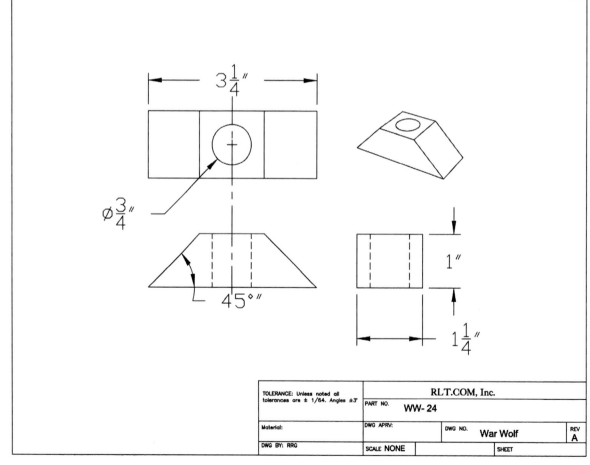

$3\frac{1}{4}''$

$\phi\frac{3}{4}''$

45°″

1″

$1\frac{1}{4}''$

TOLERANCE: Unless noted all tolerances are ± 1/64. Angles ±3°	RLT.COM, Inc.
	PART NO. WW-24
Material:	DWG APRV: / DWG NO. War Wolf / REV A
DWG BY: RRG	SCALE NONE / SHEET

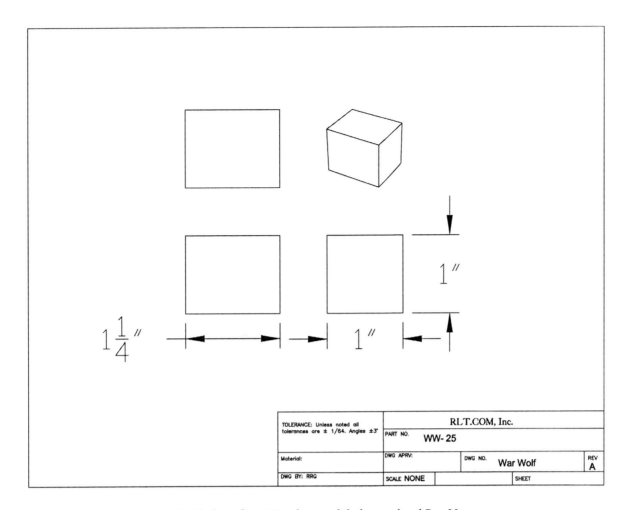

$1\frac{1}{4}''$ $1''$ $1''$

TOLERANCE: Unless noted all tolerances are ± 1/64. Angles ±3°	RLT.COM, Inc.		
	PART NO. WW- 25		
Material:	DWG APRV:	DWG NO. War Wolf	REV A
DWG BY: RRG	SCALE NONE		SHEET

Here is a listing of Part Numbers and their correlated Part Names.

WW-1 base beams	WW-14 CW bucket bottom plate
WW-2 main arm beam	WW-15 CW bucket end plates
WW-3 A-frame legs	WW-16 axle block mount plates
WW-4 trough board	WW-17 axle block plates 6" long, grooved, with two holes
WW-5 base cross beam	WW-18 axle block plates 6" long, grooved, with four holes
WW-6 vertical beams	
WW-7 short arm beams	WW-19 plywood base plate
WW-8 outrigger braces	WW-20 plywood bucket sides (6 sided)
WW-9 arm plates	WW-21 plywood bucket sides
WW-10 counterweight hangers	WW-22 main axle dowel
WW-11 side beams	WW-23 counterweight axle dowel
WW-12 base cross-braces	WW-24 arm spacers
WW-13 base cross-braces	WW-25 small block

1. The Frame

Start with the long base beam and the two cross braces with the holes in the ends. Put the long pieces on top of the short pieces to make a rectangle, then insert a 2 ½" dowel into the holes to secure it (Figure 1). Slide the long 30 ¼" crossbeam under the base beams in the center, and the other two short crossbeams under the holes (on the sides) of the base beams. We'll attach these pieces later (Figure 2).

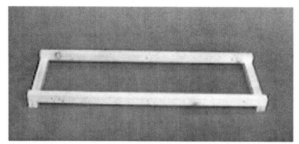

Fig. 1

Fig. 2

On one side, get a vertical beam and set it to the inside of one of the base beams, on top of the crossbeam. The two holes in the middle of the beam should be near to the top. Attach it to the base with a dowel. Make an 'A' frame with two of the A-frame beams and attach them to the base beam with dowels (they should be resting on top of the crossbeams, and again, the middle hole should be near the top- Fig. 3). Use an axle block mount plate (with three holes) to hold the top of the 'A' frame together (Fig. 4). Attach it with the 2 ½" dowel pins and some wood glue on the inside surfaces. It will seem loose right now. Do the next step before the glue sets!

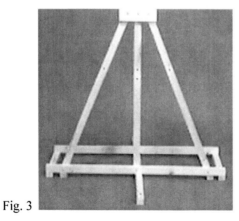

Fig. 3

Fig. 4

Fig. 5a   Fig. 5b

Put the axle block plate with 4 holes on top of the struts so that it's flush with the ends of the mount plate as shown in Fig. 5a. Do the same to the other side so you have two 'A' frame assemblies. Use the axle dowel to insure that the slots are lined up straight and level (fig. 5b), and screw the blocks into the frame. Now clamp the mount plates so the glue can set properly. This will make the top of your frame strong.

Attach the outrigger beams to the 'A' frame, then the side beams. The side beams must go on the outside of the frame. It's ok if the holes don't line up exactly. Just twist or warp the beam enough to get the dowels in. This will actually make the dowels hold better. You may need to glue the side beams in place if the dowel pins are not tight enough (Fig. 7).

Fig. 6   Fig. 7

Carefully turn the frame upside down Align the cross beams with the vertical beams and drive gold screws into the holes in the crossbeams. Make sure the base is square (90 degrees) with the cross beam (Fig. 8), and attach the plywood base plate to the bottom of the base beams using the 4 black screws (Fig. 9).

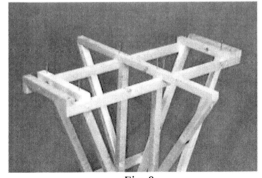

Fig. 8   fig. 9

60

Turn the frame right side up again, and place the trough board onto the frame (Fig. 10). Don't glue it down. It can be shifted to one side or the other as a crude aiming technique (Fig 11).

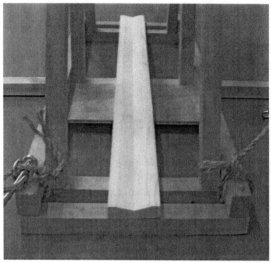

Fig 10

Fig. 11

This will finish the frame assembly! If you ever need to remove the arm and axle block assembly, you can remove the six dowel pins that hold the axle mount blocks to the frame, and lift them off.

1. The Arm

The arm is the most important part of the assembly. It must be glued together properly to make it strong. A glued joint is stronger than the wood itself if you use a good carpenter's wood glue and glue it properly.

Get the two short arm pieces with the large holes in them. Draw a line 8 inches from the ends without a hole all the way around the sides. Don't worry, this line will get covered up and won't show on the finished arm. Apply a layer of glue to one side of the wood from the end of the board to the mark you just made. Then sandwich the main arm beam between these two glue-covered surfaces, so that the end of the main arm is lined up with the marks. IMPORTANT! Make sure the pieces line up with each other or the arm might be crooked! A crooked arm can damage or destroy your machine. Adjust as necessary to make sure the holes are aligned, and the top and bottom of the arm pieces are all flush with each other.

Clamp the pieces together hard with a couple of good clamps so the glue will be forced into the pores of the wood. Let the glue set for at least an hour before removing the clamps, but don't apply any stress to the joint for at least 24 hours.

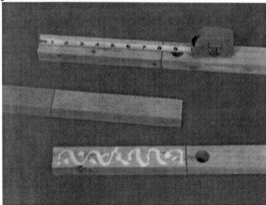

Fig. 12

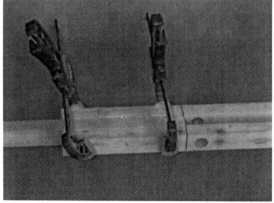

Fig. 13

Glue the small block between the short arms at the end so that it is flush with the ends of the short arms. Don't block the axle holes! Then glue the arm spacers to the sides of the arm so that the main axle holes are all aligned and the axle turns freely. If necessary, use a half-rounded file to widen the holes a little so that the axle can turn easily. Don't get any glue on the axle or on the inside surfaces of the axle holes!

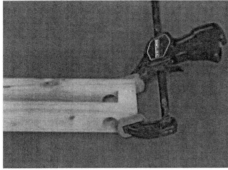

Fig. 14

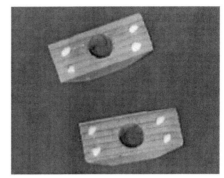

Fig. 15

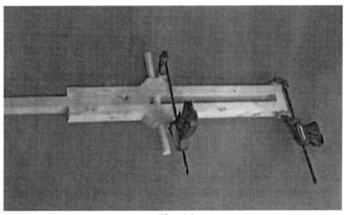

Fig. 16

Use the same gluing procedure to attach the top and bottom plates to the arm, flush with the short arms.

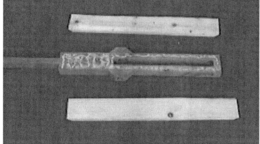

Fig. 17

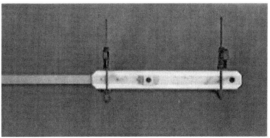

Fig. 18

Put glue in the hole at the end of the long arm beam, and insert the ½" wide dowel into the hole (Fig 19.)

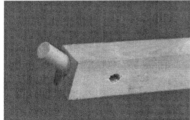

Fig. 19

Fig 20

You should now have a completed arm. Once all the glue is dry, put the main axle (11" dowel) through the arm and slide a steel ring onto each end, up against the arm (fig. 20) . Rest the axle in the channel of the block. It may be a tight fit. This is ok, the steel rings will act as a bearing and you should still get it to turn pretty easily. You can always dab a little axle grease on it too. Now put the block with only two holes on top of that. Use the pegs to secure the top block, but don't glue it. It's not necessary, and this makes it easier to remove the arm for transportation.

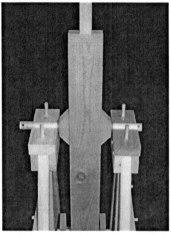
Fig. 21a

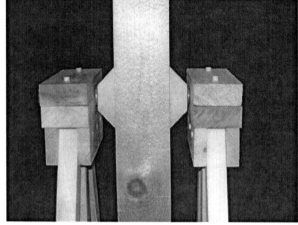
Fig. 21b

Put small dowel pins into the holes on the ends of the arms to keep it from sliding into the mount blocks.

The Counterweight Bucket

It is very important that the counterweight bucket be constructed squarely. If it is twisted or crooked, or it doesn't hang straight, it may strike the frame when firing and that can eventually destroy your machine. Be sure to double-check everything while putting the bucket together!

Start with the 4 plywood sides. Lay them together as in fig. 22.

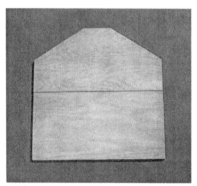
Fig. 22

Glue the counterweight hangers onto the plywood sides so that the bottom of the hanger is ¾ inch from the bottom of the plywood, and 4 ¾" from the sides. Be sure to use enough glue to cover the surface entirely, and clamp the pieces together, or set something heavy on them while the glue dries. The two sides of the bucket should be exactly the same. An easy way to check this is to hold them back-to-back with each other. While the glue is still wet, hold the side assemblies together to make sure the hangers are exactly the same length and have the same alignment. Clamp them hard so the glue will set properly, and be sure to check for any slippage after you've clamped it! The counterweight hangers **must** be properly aligned with each other, so double and triple check everything!

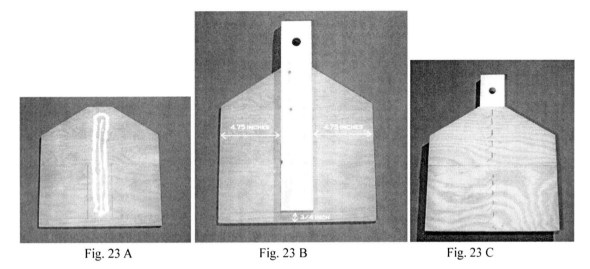

| Fig. 23 A | Fig. 23 B | Fig. 23 C |

Once the glue has set, you should nail several of the small nails into the plywood side through to the hanger for even more strength (Fig. 23 C).

Put a bead of glue near the edge of the plywood where the end plates and bottom plates will attach.

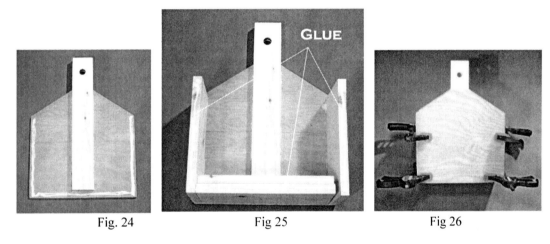

| Fig. 24 | Fig 25 | Fig 26 |

Put all the pieces together to form your counterweight box, with glue between every joint. Clamp the sides together hard to set the glue. Use as many clams as you can, or use a heavy weight to press them together. (See fig. 26) Put the axle through the counterweight hangers. Make sure that the axle spins freely and is perpendicular to the sides of the box. The bucket should hang level from the axle. The sides of the bucket must be square (90 degrees) with the axle! If this is not so, adjust the bucket while the glue is still wet Strengthen the bucket more by driving the small nails through the sides and into the plates. Don't put any nails within ½" of the ends of the plates or you might split the wood.

Assembly

Tie the base of the trigger and one steel ring to the end of the base as in Fig. 27. Be sure the slide link is on! Tie a steel ring on one end of a piece of rope (be sure the knot is STRONG!) and hook the ring into the trigger, then take the rope over the arm (in cocked position) and tie the other end of the rope to the frame on the opposite side from the trigger, as in Fig. 28. The rope should be just long enough to hold the arm down in a fully cocked position when the ring is hooked onto the trigger (Fig 29a)

Fig. 27

Fig. 28

Fig 29a

Fig. 29b

To fire the machine, tie a rope or piece of twine to the base near the trigger, carefully thread it through the trigger, over the oval slide ring, and down through the steel ring (See Fig. 29b). From a safe distance and with no people or property within 200 feet of the machine, stand well off to the side of the machine and pull the string to fire. BE CAREFUL! This is a very easy pull trigger!

Hang the counterweight bucket in place at the end of the arm. Slide the counterweight axle into place, again using a steel ring as a spacer wherever needed. Put the 3/16" dowels into the CW axle holes to keep it in place. You may need to glue the 3/16" dowels. Put the white poly sand bag inside of the counterweight bucket. Fill the bag with your counterweight material, and tie the top of the bag closed so the material won't spill out when the bucket swings around. You can fill it up now, but DO NOT fire the machine without a missile! This is a called a dry-fire, and it will damage your machine! Always have an appropriately balanced missile in the sling for the amount of counterweight you are using. See the section on tuning for more info.

Fig. 30

Fig. 31

5. The sling

Cut a piece of the burlap about 8" x 12" and lay it flat. Fold two sides over so they touch in the center, making a strip 12" x 4" double thick (**A**). Then fold the edges of this strip (lengthwise) up (**B**), then in half back down (**C**) to form an 'M' shape. Turn this over so the 'M' is now a 'W' (**D**).

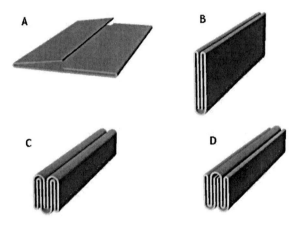

Fig. 32

Tie each end **tight** with the rope about 2" from each end of the sling pouch so that the knot is on the top of the 'W'. Fold the loose ends of the pouch around the knot and secure them tightly with another piece of rope or twine. You may even want to glue the knots so they won't come open. If the pouch is not secured well, it can slip off the sling during firing. Push the center of the 'W' inside out (through the bottom, see Fig 33) and you should be left with a perfect sling-pouch (Fig 34).

Fig. 33

Now cut the rope 40" from each end of the sling. Tie one end through the hole in the end of the arm so that the knot is on the bottom side of the arm (Fig. 35). Tie a steel ring to the other end of the sling, and put the ring over the pin. With the arm horizontal make sure that the sling-pouch hangs properly and cradles a ball about 2" to 4" in diameter about 32 inches from the ring to the sling pouch. If one side of the sling is too long, you can just tie knots in the rope to make it shorter. This also gives you the opportunity to lengthen the sling if needed by simply untying the knots! (You may want to make it a bit longer if you want to fine-tune the sling length for maximum range -see the section on tuning).

Fig. 34   Fig. 35

6. Firing the machine.

Pick a spot that is flat and level to set the machine on. Pull the arm down and set the trigger. BE VERY CAREFUL! The trigger is very easy to release! Stay clear of the path of the arm and counterweight, and put the sling's steel ring over the pin and pull the sling back into the trough so that the lines are not twisted. Fig. 36

Fig 36.

The pouch goes over and under the ball, not around its sides. Verify that the sling loop is still on the pin. Make sure there is nothing for 200 feet in front of or in back of the machine! A trebuchet that hasn't been tuned can just as easily throw something backwards, forwards, or even straight up! Perhaps you should wear a hardhat too! With the machine aimed, stand at least 6 feet away from the side of the trebuchet. Pull the trigger string slowly (do not 'jerk' the string) until it releases. Then watch it fly!

Always remember that the arm moves very fast and with a lot of power behind it! It can knock you out if it hits your head. NEVER stand over, in front of or behind a cocked machine, whether it is loaded or not! Never fire it at any person or thing. The trebuchet should only be fired into an open field and under strict adult supervision.

7. Tuning the machine.

A trebuchet can be a slightly complicated thing to tune properly. There are a lot of variables that all affect each other. Things that you can easily tune are: The counterweight, The projectile weight, The sling length

The first thing most people think is that increasing the counterweight will make the machine throw farther. It might, a little. It might also make the trebuchet throw backwards or straight up, or you might just create more stress on the machine and break something. More counterweight usually only allows you to throw a comparably heavier projectile. Doubling your counterweight should mean that you can double the weight of your projectile and get the same performance. If the projectile is too light in relation to the tuning of the machine, it will probably come out of the sling at the wrong time.

More counterweight means that you have more power. To convert that power into more range, you'll need to adjust a few other things. Changing the counterweight without a corresponding change in the projectile weight will probably require a little additional tuning of the sling length.

Note: Do not "dry-fire" the machine (firing with no projectile loaded)
We recommend these ratios:
 For a ¼ lb missile, use 15 to 20 lbs of counterweight.
For a ½ lb missile, use 20 to 30 lbs of counterweight.
For a 1 lb or greater missile, use 30 to 50 lbs of counterweight. Use NO MORE than 50 lbs of counterweight. Too much weight may cause your counterweight bucket to shatter.
Do not hurl any missiles greater than 1.5 lbs.

The sling length:
Watch the missile very carefully while firing the machine. If it flies in a high lob, the sling probably needs to be shorter. To make it shorter you can just tie knots in both sides of the sling. This is a great way to make fine adjustments in the sling length. If the missile flies low to the ground and not very far, a longer sling should make it fly higher, and therefore farther.

See page 44 for information on calculating your range efficiency.

Section Three:
Torsion and Tension Machines

The RAT TRAP spoon-a-pult (catapult) plans

WARNING!

This is a potentially dangerous project. Rat Traps are capable of extremely fast action with a lot of force (hey, it can catch and kill a rat!) While we've never had a mishap with our rat trap catapult models, we cannot be responsible for the suitability of rat traps in general, nor of the other components in this model. In fact, we specifically state that all the components of this project, including the rat trap, the spoon, the tape, twine and 2x4 board are not intended for this kind of project, and the result can be unpredictable and is most likely very dangerous. If you choose to build one of these models, you do so entirely at your own risk. By building a model based on these plans, you agree that you are doing so at your own risk, and that you will not hold RLT Industries or any of its employees or principles liable for any damages or injuries that may occur as a result of the construction or use of this model.

Why do we call it a "spoon-a-pult"

Hollywood loves the catapult with a spoon on the end of the arm, and for good reason, most of the historical drawings you see of catapults are equipped with spoon-arms. But, ask an historian, and he'll tell you that real catapults didn't have spoons. They had slings on the end of that arm.

All of those drawings are simply artists impressions from the late Middle Ages and more recently than that, not actual historical details. These drawings were produced well into the era of gunpowder and cannons, so what's up with the drawings?

You wouldn't expect the US Military to publish detailed plans of their most advanced weapons systems, and the same thinking was true in ancient times. The catapults of the Greeks and Romans were military secrets, not to be shared or discussed in the open. That they existed was well known, but the details of their construction, including drawings, were probably not allowed. And since they were already rare and controlled-access documents, none have survived the ages.

In battle, it's not uncommon for the losing side to intentionally sabotage their weaponry in order to prevent them from falling into enemy hands. Ships are intentionally sunk, guns are broken to pieces, and information is burned. So too were the catapults.

But there do exist scant few descriptions of them and their operation from ancient times. And there have been a great many experimental reconstructions of catapults based on those descriptions. From this information, we know that a spoon-arm catapult is nowhere near as effective as a sling-arm catapult. In battle, more effective weapons usually mean victory. For this reason, it is most likely that all true catapults were sling-arm machines, and not "spoon-a-pults". But hey, a spoon-a-pult can still be fun and educational too! So let's build one.

Materials you will need to build a Rat Trap catapult:

1. a Rat trap. (Not a mousetrap! Rattraps are considerably bigger than mousetraps, and are usually sold in packages of one. Mousetraps are usually sold in packages of three. Here's what a rattrap package looks like:

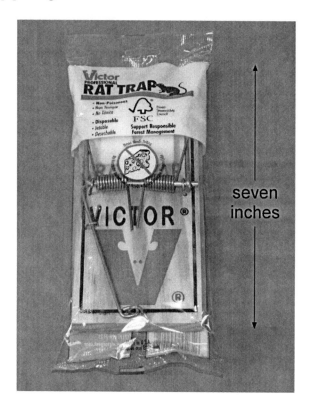

2. A 2x4 board, about two feet long.
3. Strapping tape. A good, strong strapping tape (the kind with fibers running it's length)
4. Twine, about two feet should do.
5. A tablespoon. Metal, shaped from flat plate stock so you can bend it.
6. A rubber ball.

Tools you will need:

1. Pliers - preferably needle nose, but any will do.
2. A light hammer

Construction:

First we'll need to modify the rattrap a little.
Open the package and familiarize yourself with the components of a rattrap. There's usually a staple holding the trigger lock-down bar in place. You'll need to remove this staple.

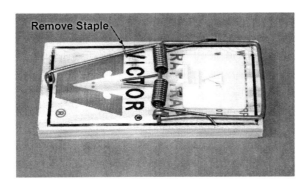

The first thing we'll do is un-hook the spring legs from the bow, and raise the bow.

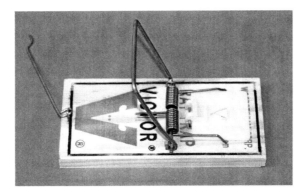

The springs are probably going to be close to the center of the spring-axle, so we need to spread them apart. Move the springs toward the sides of the rat-trap.

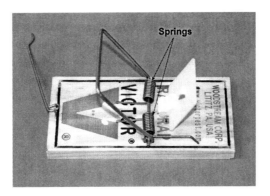

As it is, the rattrap is too lightweight to remain stable if it's used to throw anything, so we have to attach it to a heavier base. A 2x4 board is perfect. The length doesn't matter, as long as it's at least 2 feet long. Use strapping tape to attach the rattrap to the 2x4 board near one end, so the front of the rattrap is about four inches from the end of the board. (I used blue tape in the photo to show up better. You should use strapping tape.)

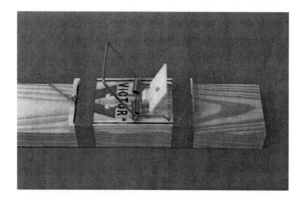

The trigger bar needs to be moved from the center of the trap to one side. Using pliers, pull out the staple holding the trigger bar. Be careful to note which way the trigger bar goes in the staple. Re-attach the trigger bar staple one inch to one side, and 1/8 of an inch forward (towards the center). It is important to move the staple forwards a bit so that the latch will still catch on the trigger bar when it's off-center like this.

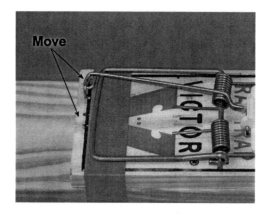

Once you've moved the trigger bar staple, use the hammer to drive it into the wood. Make sure it is firmly attached! Check that the trigger bar will still engage the plastic latch and that the latch will release it when depressed. If it doesn't you can bend the staple forward to make it reach farther, or bend the trigger bar a little to reduce its length.

The rattrap is almost ready. Now it's time to work on the spoon.

You'll need to bend a loop, or hook in the spoon. The location of this loop is important. Measure the distance from the spring axle to the bow.

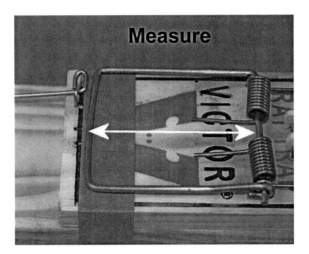

Now, this is important- the tip of your spoon handle must be able to fit under the spring axle. This will be part of the leverage system in your catapult, so you'll need to inspect your spoon to determine how your spoon will fit. In my case, the last 1/4" of the spoon fit well under the axle, so I added 1/4" to the measurement above to determine the location where to bend my spoon. Don't put too much handle under the axle, or it will dig into the wood as it rotates over the trap. Be sure to check (rotate the spoon and bow over the trap) to see if it digs into the wood. Here's how my spoon fits:

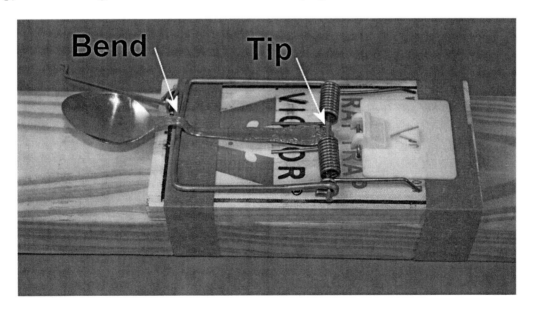

Here's the spoon by itself so you can see the bend. The bend will rest on the bow and keep the spoon in place, so make it as form fitting and as accurate as possible.

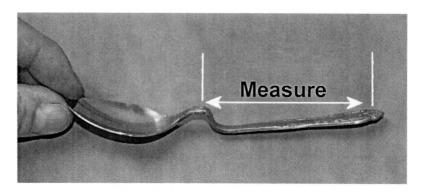

Now that the spoon is shaped properly, attach it to the rattrap bow. Fold the bow over to the front of the trap, and slide the spoon under the bow so that the tip rests on top of the spring axle. This position will make it easier to tie the spoon to the bow.

Tie the spoon onto the bow with the twine. Use a good criss-cross pattern so that the spoon will not slip!

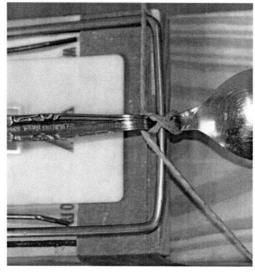

The completed catapult:

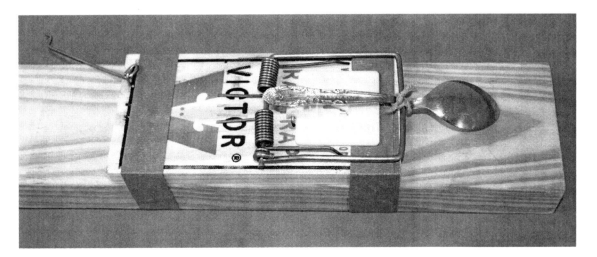

Cocking and firing the machine:

To cock the rat-trap catapult, pull the spoon all the way back and set the trigger as usual for a rat-trap. Be sure to keep all fingers, face, and other body parts well away. Be aware that the spoon could come loose and be flung across the room, so make sure there are no people or breakable objects anywhere near the machine, and make sure everyone is aware of what's happening and the potential dangers involved.

The cocked machine:

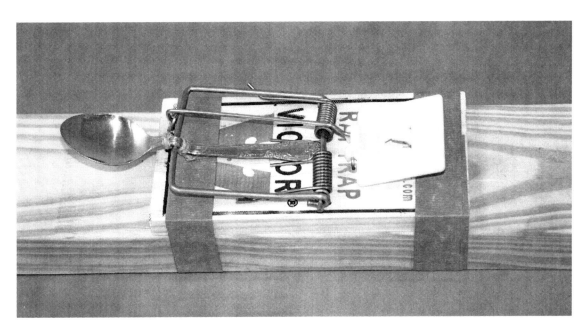

Make sure there is nothing within 50 feet of the front of the machine, and carefully and gently place the rubber ball in the spoon.

The cocked and loaded machine:

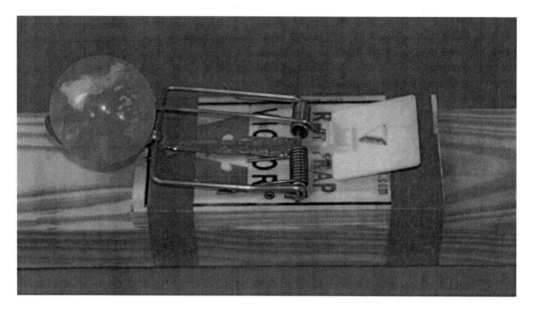

Stand back. Use a long stick to press down on the plastic trigger pad, and watch that ball fly! Heavy balls (tennis balls, large rubber balls, etc.) will only go a few feet, but lightweight balls (small rubber balls, small wooden balls, marbles, etc.) will fly very far-up to 50 feet, and can hit with considerable force.

Only use the rattrap catapult outdoors, in open spaces, with strict and competent adult supervision at all times.

Suggested Experiments:

Hurl an item 100 times, and measure the impact point for each throw. Do you see a pattern to the impact points? What can you deduce about the machine based on the impact pattern?

Hurl ten different items with different weights, and measure the distance to the impact points. How do the measurements compare to the weights? Is there a constant multiple you can derive to predict how far an item will go based on its weight?

Change the angle of the spoon (bend it a little bit). So that it angles up a bit. What affect does this have on the projectiles? What if the spoon is angled down?

Put the front end of the catapult on a block to tilt the whole machine back a bit (instead of angling just the spoon). Does this yield a different result than angling just the spoon? What if you put the block on the back of the machine, so it tilts forward?

How much does the shape of the payload affect the range and flight path? Try round, square, cylindrical, and other odd shapes. To get an accurate test, they should all be about the same size and the same weight.

The Mighty Roman Mangonel

Parts list:

Hardware:

1 square-bend hook screw	15 feet of twine	20 wood screws, 1-5/8" long
1 eye-screw	2 split rings	2 large flat washers
1 D-shaped ring	2 steel dowel pins	1 steel trigger hook
1 round ring		12 small nails

Wooden parts:

2 base side beams 18" long	2 strut beams, 12" long, tip-to-tip
2 brace blocks 5 ½" long x 2 3/8" wide	2 strike beams, 5 ½" long x 1 ¼" wide
1 brace block 5 ½" long, angled cut	1 arm pole (oval) 14" long.
2 verticle beams 11 ½" long.	1 winch dowel 10" long
2 skein anchor blocks	4 feet, 4 inches long tip-to-tip
2 - ¼" wood dowels 2 ½" long	6 - 5/16" wood dowels 2" long

Other Parts:
1 length of nylon rope, 3/8" diameter and 30 feet long should do.
1 strip of stiff leather, 1" wide and 10 inches long.
1 swatch of soft leather, 2" x 4" minimum.

Tools you will need:
1. A Phillips-head screwdriver (#2 size will work for all screws)
2. A carpenter's square, or any good 90 degree reference.
3. Scissors
4. A good wood glue.
5. Two clamps capable of spanning 3 inches.
6. A light hammer
7. (optional) a crochet hook for threading the skein
8. (optional) a lighter or matches for fusing the nylon rope ends.
9. (optional) Sandpaper for smoothing any rough edges or tight fitting pieces.

Hardware: You'll be able to get most of this stuff from any hardware store. Other things you might be able to find around the house or on-line.

15 feet of twine – nylon mason's twine or hemp twine work best. Kite string is also fine.

1 steel trigger hook – You'll have to make this out of stiff wire, or cut one from 1/8" plate steel. There's a drawing at the end of this document.

2 large flat washers – fender washers, 1" size hole, 2 inch diameter to the outside edge.

1 eye-screw 1/2" long.

1 square bend hook screws – also known as an L-hook. it's a screw that has a 90 degree bend in it and no head.

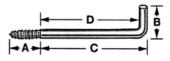

A = 11/16", B = 3/4", C = 1-9/16"

1 steel ring – ½" inside diameter. We DO NOT recommend using split key rings. These rings are made of brittle metal, and can shatter under certain conditions. This ring may experience impact loads up to 50 pounds.

D-ring: 1" at the base (C):

Split key rings for attaching the trigger to the haul-down line. Inside diameter about 5/8".

Steel dowel pins: 3/8" diameter and 3.5" long.

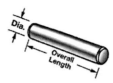

Wood screws: #6 size works best, 1-5/8" long. You'll need 20 of these.

Part number: TRIGGER

edge view   side view

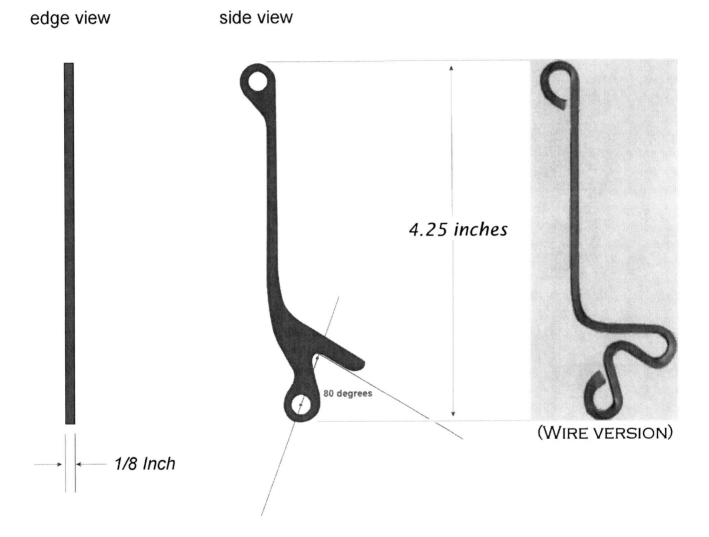

4.25 inches

1/8 Inch

80 degrees

(WIRE VERSION)

Piece number 1

Quantity: 2

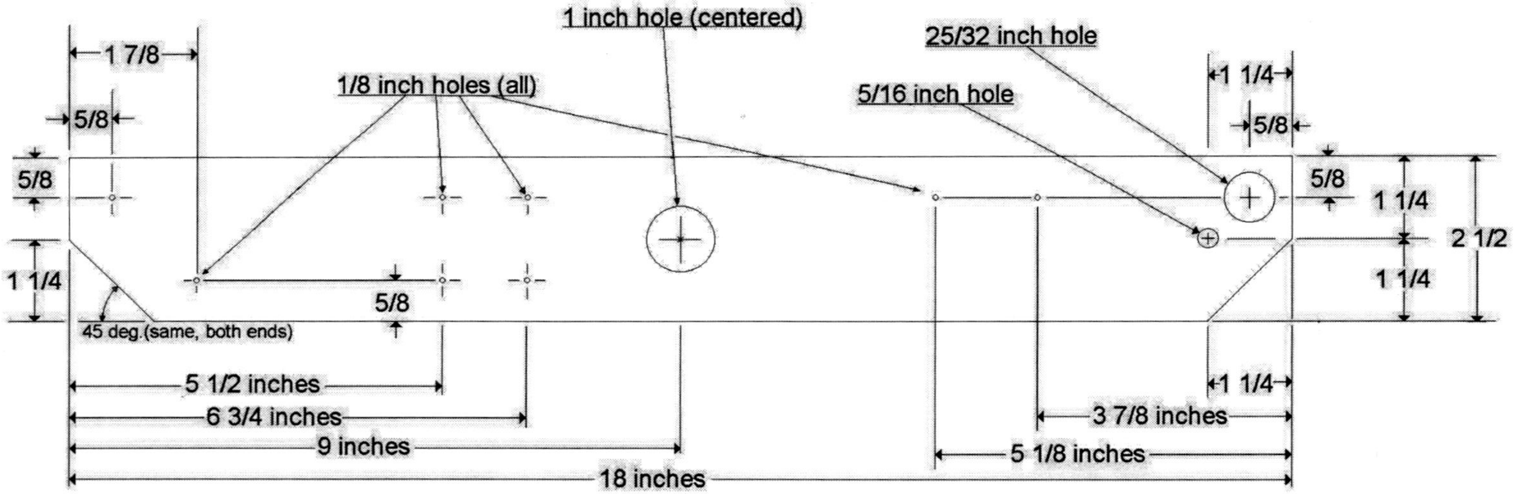

2 1/2

1 1/4

1 1/4

5/8

5/8

1 1/4

25/32 inch hole

5/16 inch hole

1 1/4

1 1/4

3 7/8 inches

5 1/8 inches

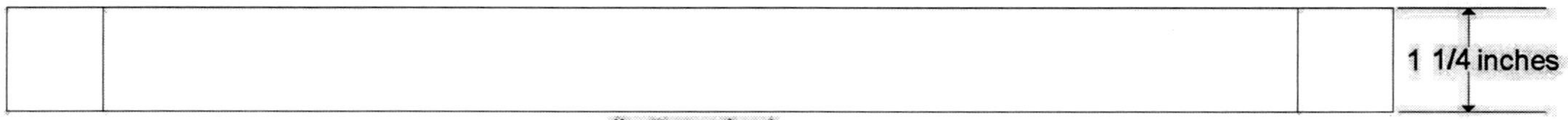

1 inch hole (centered)

1/8 inch holes (all)

5/8

18 inches

5 1/2 inches

6 3/4 inches

9 inches

1 7/8

5/8

5/8

1 1/4

45 deg (same, both ends)

1 1/4 inches

1 1/4 inches

(bottom view)

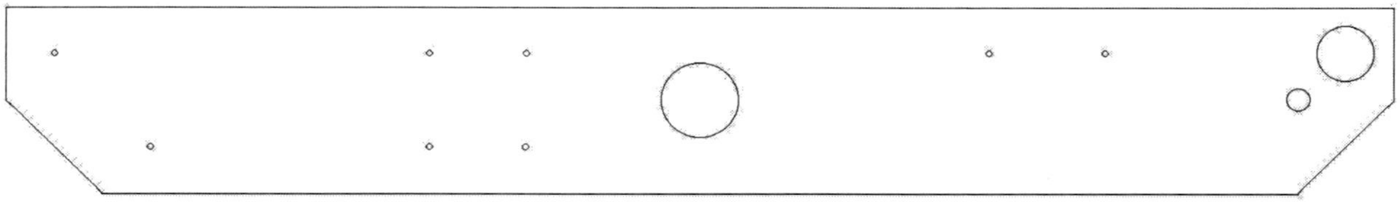

(finished piece)

81

Part number 2
Quantity: 1

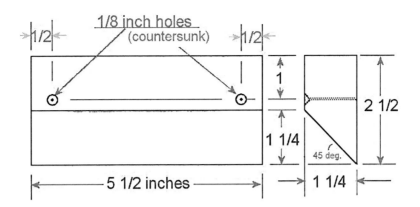

Part number 3
Quantity: 2

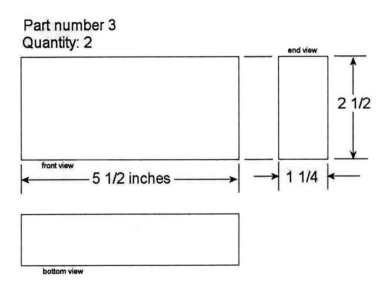

Part number 4
Quantity: 4

(angles are 45 deg.
on both ends.)

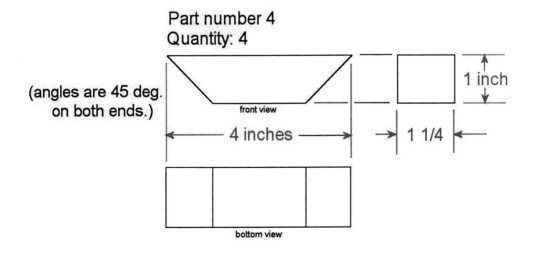

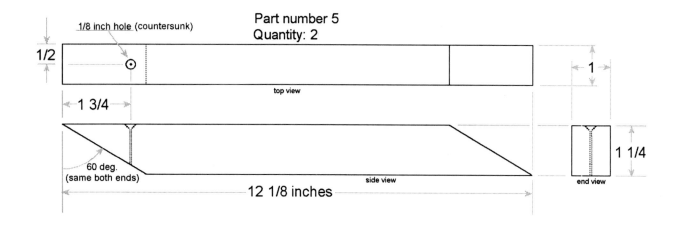

Part number 5
Quantity: 2

1/8 inch hole (countersunk)

1/2

1 3/4

top view

1

60 deg.
(same both ends)

12 1/8 inches

side view

end view

1 1/4

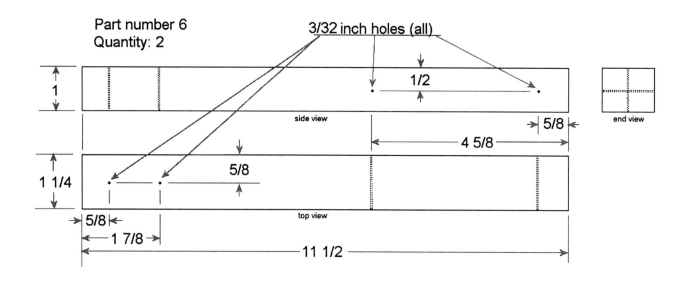

Part number 6
Quantity: 2

3/32 inch holes (all)

1

1/2

side view

5/8

4 5/8

end view

1 1/4

5/8

top view

5/8

1 7/8

11 1/2

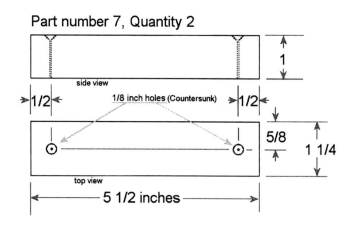

Part number 7, Quantity 2

1

side view

1/2

1/8 inch holes (Countersunk)

1/2

5/8

1 1/4

top view

5 1/2 inches

Part number 8
Quantity: 2

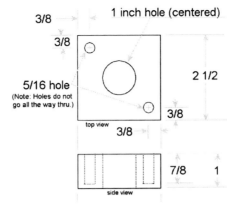

3/8

1 inch hole (centered)

3/8

5/16 hole
(Note: Holes do not
go all the way thru.)

2 1/2

3/8

top view

3/8

7/8   1

side view

Part number 9
Quantity: 1

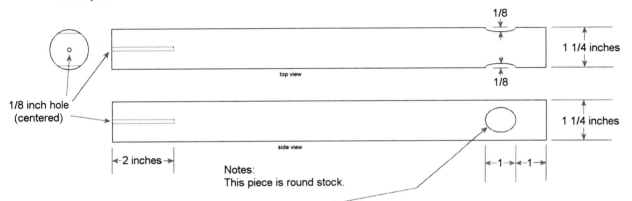

1/8

1 1/4 inches

top view

1/8

1/8 inch hole
(centered)

1 1/4 inches

side view

2 inches

1   1

Notes:
This piece is round stock.

This is not a hole.
It is a shallow cut-out on opposite sides of the part.
The shape of the cut-out is not important, as long as it is 1/8 inch deep and 1 inch long (as shown).

Part number 10
Quantity: 1

1/4 inch hole   (all)

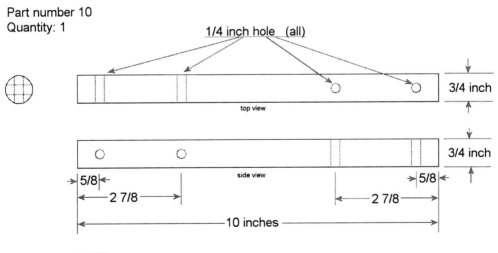

3/4 inch

top view

3/4 inch

side view

5/8

5/8

2 7/8

2 7/8

10 inches

NOTE:
This piece is round stock.

Assembly Instructions:

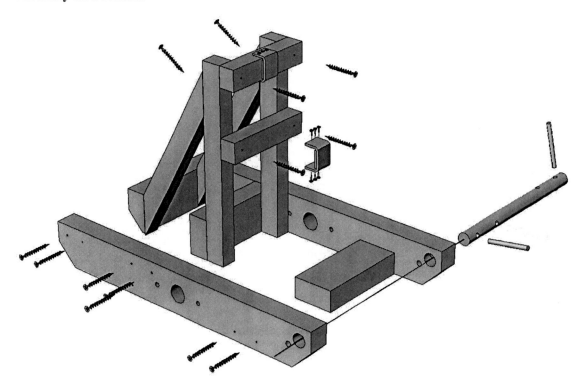

Before you build the mangonel, you might try to stain the wood. But don't do it just yet! It's better to wait until after the frame is assembled, otherwise the stain will prevent the glue from working properly.

Building the frame:

Start with the two large side beams. The end with the ¾" hole (not the hole in the middle) will go to the rear of the machine. Pick the beam that will go on the left side. On the inside face of the beam, make a mark 6 ¼ inches from the front, and draw a line from top to bottom. Make sure the line is square to the top and bottom of the beam. Don't worry, this line won't show when you're done. Do the same thing to the right side beam.

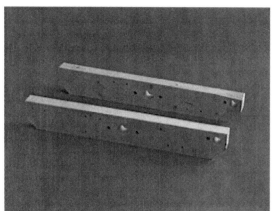
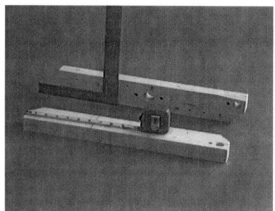

Fig. 1   Fig. 2

Glue one end of a square brace block flush with the line on the beam, on the side of the line away from the center hole (see fig. 4). Make sure the piece is flush with the mark you made, and that it is square with the sides. Drive two black screws into the side to hold the brace in place. Sink them into the wood till the screws are flush with the surface of the wood (Fig. 5). It's important to glue AND screw these braces so the frame will be doubly strong. There will be a lot of pressure and impact on these pieces when you fire the machine!

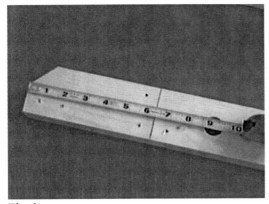

Fig. 3

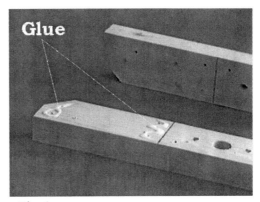

Fig. 4

Do the same thing with the angle-cut front brace, making it flush to the front end of the side beam.

Fig. 5

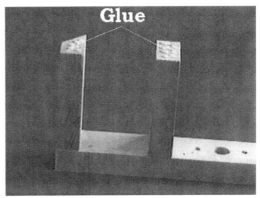

Fig. 6

Put glue on the other ends of the braces (Fig. 6) and attach the right side beam, being sure to align it with the line you made and check that it is square (90 degrees). Attach with two black screws.

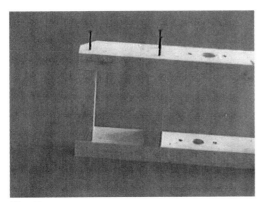

Fig. 7

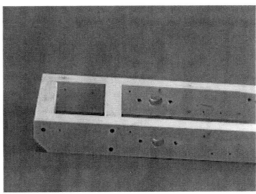

Fig. 8

The last cross-brace won't be absorbing any impact, so it doesn't need glue. Slide it in between the side beams flush with the bottom of the frame, and attach it with the black screws.

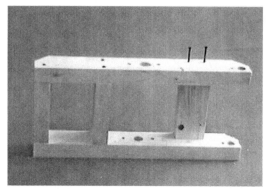

Fig. 9

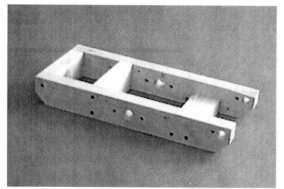

fig. 10

The Vertical beams:

The two 11 ½ inch vertical beams should be glued to the inside of the frame. They must be placed in front of the cross brace (between the brace and the large center hole of the side beams) with the broad face of the vertical beam against the side beams. Glue it to both surfaces. Use a carpenter's square to make sure they are 90 degrees to the side beams and clamp into place (fig. 12, 11). Then drive a black screw into each piece through the side beams. Once the black screws are secure you can remove the clamps.

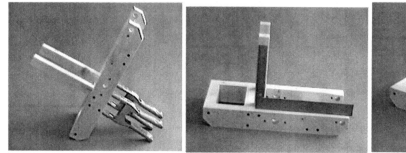

Fig. 11   Fig. 12   Fig. 13

The Struts:

The angled struts go on next. The end with the pre-drilled hole in it goes towards the top. They should be glued on each end, and attached with a black screw at the front of the frame first, then, making sure that the vertical beams are still 90 degrees to the side beams, drive a screw through the strut (in the pre-drilled hole) and into the vertical beam to hold it in place.

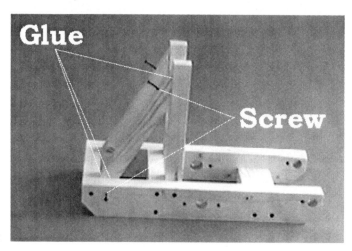

Fig. 14:

87

It is very important that you glue the frame together properly. The screws alone are not strong enough to hold the struts in place after repeated firings.

The last two frame pieces, the arm strike beams, will go on later after the skein has been tensioned. Don't put them on now or you'll have a harder time tensioning your skein!

Now is a good time to stain all the wood.

The Winch:

Slide the ¾" dowel into the holes at the back of the frame. The kit was manufactured in Southern California, which is a very dry environment. If you live in a place with higher humidity, the dowels may have swelled and will seem very tight. You may need to file the holes a little bigger in this case. If the winch dowel is hard to turn, scrape a pencil lead all over the surfaces that make contact. Pencil lead is made from graphite, and it's a great way to lubricate things that need to stay dry. People have been using graphite for lubrication for centuries!

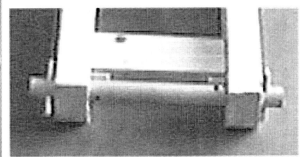

fig. 15   fig. 16

Slide the ¼" pegs through the holes on the winch dowel outside the frame (fig. 16). The holes on the inside will be used to hold the rope later.

Put two of the 5/16" pegs into the holes in the frame next to the winch. These should be able to slide in and out of the frame, so don't glue them! (Use the graphite to make them slide easier)

The Arm:

If you are staining your machine, the arm should be stained before you assemble it.

The arm is probably the most important part of the machine. If it's not assembled properly, it may break after repeated use. If it ever does break, we have replacement parts available. Just email us for more information. The arm has an oval cross section. This helps to keep it in the right orientation in the rope skein, and the force of hitting the strike pads is distributed better.

First screw the angled hook screw into the end of the arm. Screw it in until the hook is about ½ inch from the end of the arm (fig. 18). Point the hook towards one of the flatter sides of the arm.

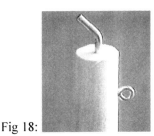
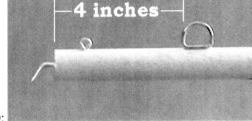

Fig 18:   Fig 20:

Now screw the small eye screw into the arm on the side of the arm opposite where the hook is pointing, as in fig. 20. The eye screw should be 1 inch from the tip of the arm. DO NOT tie the sling directly to the eye. The eye-screw is only intended to prevent the sling from slipping up or down the arm after repeated firings. We'll talk more about the sling later.

Glue the D-ring onto the side of the arm below the eye-screw so that the top of the D-ring is 4 inches from the top of the arm (fig 20). The glue is not actually going to hold this in place, so don't use a lot of it. Gluing the D-ring in place is only done to make the next step a lot easier.

Wrapping the arm:

This is a technique for wrapping a cord around wood to make it stronger and possibly keep it from breaking under stress. It is very strong and it's also how we will secure the winch hook (D-ring) and sling to the arm.

Here's the basic technique for wrapping-

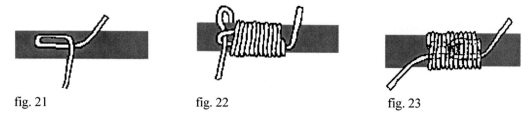

fig. 21   fig. 22   fig. 23

1. Make a loop against your beam (fig. 21).
2. Wrap the cord around the beam and over the loop. Be sure to keep the cord as tight as you can during this process (fig.22).
3. Insert the loose end of the cord through the open loop (make it a tight wrap) then pull the loose end under the wrapping using the other loose end (fig 23). On some types of cord you can just cut the ends and leave it at that, but nylon tends to slip, so bring the loose ends together over the wrapping and tie them together. You may want to practice this a couple of times before you make it permanent.

Start about ½" below the D-ring, and wrap the arm all the way up to at least ½" above the D-ring. Pass the cord through the ring as you wind it up (figs. 24, 25). The most important thing is to keep the windings as tight as possible.

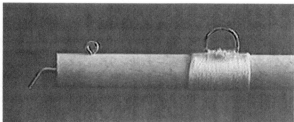

fig. 24   fig. 25

The sling:

Poke 4 holes in each end of the pouch leather about 3/4" from the end, like this:

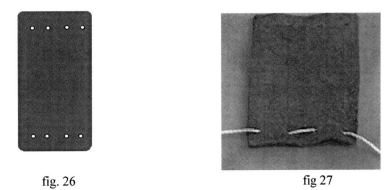

fig. 26   fig 27

Thread a string through the holes (fig. 27) and fold the leather into an M shape (figs. 28, 29, 30) and pull the string tight through the holes. Then wrap the string once around the bottom of the M, back up to the top and tie it securely at the top of the M. Use a good square knot and fuse the ends (fig 31).

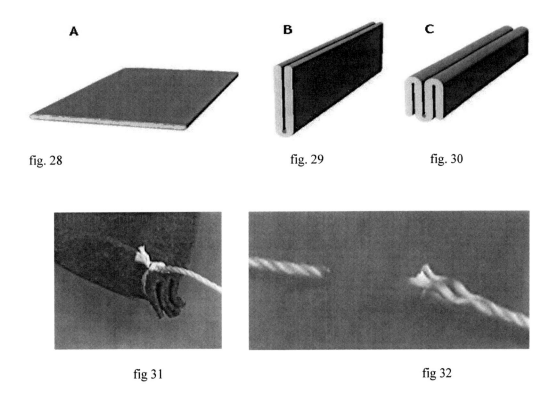

A   **B**   **C**

fig. 28   fig. 29   fig. 30

fig 31   fig 32

Fusing:

Fusing is a technique used on nylon and poly ropes to melt the end of the string and prevent it from unraveling. You can even melt the end into a small button making it almost impossible to slip through a knot. In the photo (Fig. 32), the end on the right is not fused, but the end on the left is. Do this by holding the end near a small flame just until it begins to melt. But don't catch the string on fire!

On one end of the sling-pouch, cut the string about 6 inches long and tie a loop in the end. Then slide the loop through and over the steel ring so that the ring is 4 inches from the pouch (It's ok if it's a little bit over 4 inches, we'll tell you how to shorten it later). Your finished pouch should look like fig. 37.

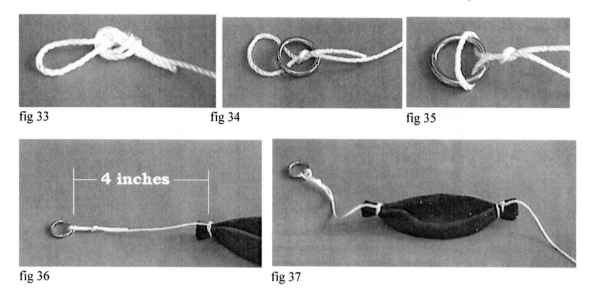

fig 33   fig 34   fig 35

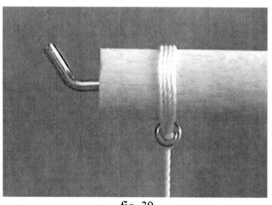

fig 36   fig 37

On the other end of the sling, cut the string about 24 inches long. This end will attach to the arm. This is very important! Don't just tie the string to the eye-screw. If you do this, the eye-screw will just rip out of place. It's only there to keep the sling from sliding off the end of the arm during firing.

Tie a knot in the long sling string so that the knot is the same length from the pouch as the steel ring is on the other string, about 4 inches. Thread the long string through the eye-screw, and wrap it three or four times around the arm, passing it through the eye-screw each time (see fig. 38). Tie and fuse the end of the string. Be sure that you only heat the ends! If you heat the knots or any other part of the string, you'll weaken it and it may break.

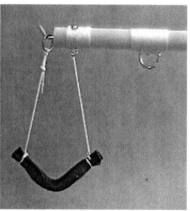

fig. 39   fig. 38

Then wrap the arm with another piece of string starting from ½" below the eye-screw, all the way up to within ½" of the end of the arm. This will help to prevent the end of the arm from splitting. Be sure to get the wraps tight! When you get to the eye-screw wraps, just pass the string through the eye and continue wrapping on the other side of the sling wraps.

Here's what your completed arm should look like. (See fig. 39. Actually, you should wrap **a lot** closer to the tip of the arm than we did for this photo.)

The skein:

This is the source of power for your machine. The more powerful you want your machine to be, the more difficult it will be to build the skein. For easy construction and a machine that can throw golf balls about 40 feet, use 4 loops on the skein (4 strands on top of the arm, and 4 on bottom). To shoot a golf ball over 80 feet, we used 9 wraps on our model. The more wraps you use, the harder it will be to tension the skein, and the harder it will be to cock the machine when firing. Using too much tension will damage the machine, so don't go crazy!

Put the large metal plate rings over the side holes on the outside of the frame, and lay the capstans over these plates centered over the holes. Putting the machine upside down and using clamps to hold everything together will make this easier (Fig. 40).

Tie one end of the nylon rope to a vertical beam, and pass it through the skein hole from outside the frame. Thread it the same on both capstans- bottom-to-bottom, then top-to-top, etc. After you get one or two wraps in, put the arm in the bundle so that it keeps the bottom wraps separate from the top wraps of each loop (Fig. 41).

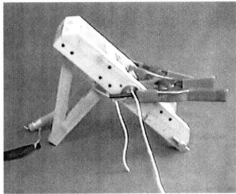 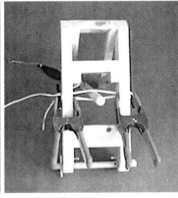 

| fig. 40 | fig 41 | fig 43 |

If you're having trouble getting the rope past the other loops and through the holes, a large crochet needle will help, or you can make a loop from a clothes hanger wire to help pull through the rope ends.

Once you've got all your loops in place, untie the rope from the vertical beam and tie the ends of the rope together in a secure square knot over the capstan (fig. 44). Fuse the ends so it won't slip out. Slide the arm up so its bottom end is about 1 inch from the skein. Your model should look like fig. 45

fig 44　　　　　　　　fig 45

Your skein should already be pre-tensioned. Don't worry if you didn't get it very tight. Just wind it up more during this phase. The base of the arm should stick out about 1 inch from the skein bundle, and make sure it is facing the right way (with the D-ring to the back and the pin pointing forward) before you tension the skein.

Use a crescent wrench, vice-grips or some other device to turn the capstan towards the vertical beams (fig. 46). Make only a ¼ turn on each side at a time, then do the other side. Otherwise the arm will not stay centered. Keep the capstans in place between turns using the 5/16" wooden pegs inserted into the holes on the frame.

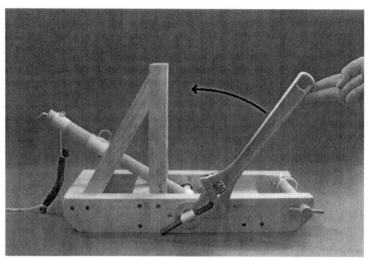

fig. 46

How many turns to use will depend on how many loops you have and how much tension (if any) is already in the skein. At least one full turn is usually enough, but use two full turns if you have to. It should be hard to turn. The harder it is to turn, the more force you are storing in the twist. But don't over-tighten it or you'll start to deform the frame.

If the capstans start to bend or the steel ring-plates begin to buckle, you're turning too hard! (We did this to one of our models- it still works, but the arm cracked after only 3 firings)

Your completed skein should look something like fig. 47. (We used 5 loops in this photo)

fig 47

fig 48

The strike pads and beams:

Take the thick leather strip and cut two pieces 3 inches long, and two more pieces one inch long. Use the small black nails to attach one end of a 3" strip to the top of a strike beam (fig. 49). Then put a 1" piece of leather on the face of the strike beam, and wrap the 3" piece around the face and over the 1" pad. Nail the 3" piece to the bottom of the strike beam so it looks like fig. 50. Don't put any nails in the face of the pad, or it will probably cause the arm to crack.

fig 49

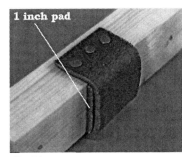

fig 50

Do this to both strike beams. Now pull the arm back (you might need a friend to hold the base steady while you do this) and place one of the strike beams between the arm and the vertical beams so that the strike beam is flush with the top of the vertical beams (fig. 51). The arm will hold it in place while you attach it with the screws. Then attach the second strike beam so that it is 4 inches below the first strike beam, from top to top.

fig 51

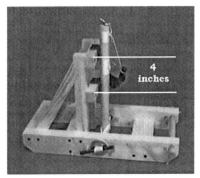

fig 52

The Feet:

By now you may notice that the capstan rods are protruding past the bottom of the side beams. If yours is not, then you don't need to install the feet (there are other reasons you may want to do this anyway). If your capstans are preventing your model from resting evenly on the floor, then glue the four feet to the bottom of the side beams as in fig. 53

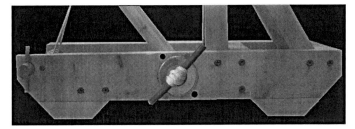

Fig. 53.

This will also make the machine sit taller, which means you can make the sling a little longer. A longer sling may give the machine more range! If you want maximum range from your machine, you should install the feet as shown.

The trigger:

Install two split rings onto the bottom loop of the trigger. Be sure to use both split rings for extra strength. Then hook the trigger onto the pull-down ring on the arm, as in fig. 55. Cut a piece of rope 26 inches long and thread it through the split rings and the holes in the winch rod (see fig. 57). You should tie a knot in the ends of the rope so it won't slip through.

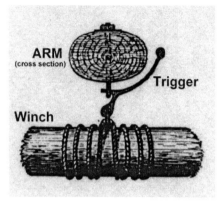

fig 54

Fig 55.

Tie a string at least 6 feet long to the top loop of the trigger and you'll be ready to go! Fig. 54 is an image from the book The projectile throwing engines of the ancients, by Ralph Payne-Gallwey, published in 1905

Cocking and firing:

Carefully wind the arm down with the winch. Be sure to stay low and well behind the machine when winding the winch! NEVER stand with your head or any part of your body over the arm! When the trigger's rings are almost touching the winch rod, it is fully cocked. Slide one of the 5/16" pegs into the closest hole to the winch handles to hold it in place. You now have a live machine, so be careful!

To fire the machine, put the sling ring on the pin at the end of the arm, and place your projectile in the sling pouch. You should never "dry fire" the machine without any projectile in the pouch. This can damage your machine and may even break the arm.

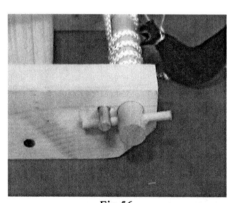

Fig 56.

fig 57

Secure the mangonel to the ground somehow- we use tent stakes to hold ours in place. Then make sure there's nothing, and especially no people in front of the machine or behind it for at least 150 feet. Let everyone in the area know what's about to happen, stand off to the side and pull the cord!

Tuning:

There are two easy ways to tune the machine, and two very hard ways.

The easiest way is to adjust the pin angle. A shallow angle will throw a flatter trajectory, and a wider angle will throw higher. Between 30 to 40 degrees is best. Set the pin angle only once. If you change it too much, the pin will break and you'll need to replace it.

The next easiest way to tune the machine is to adjust the sling length. In our test models we adjusted the sling so that it rests on the ground a little when the machine is fully cocked. You can easily shorten the sling by tying knots in the strings, like this:

Fig. 58:

To lengthen the sling, just untie some of the knots, or make a new sling. Some people get better performance with a sling about 2/3 the length of the arm. But this means that you'll have to dig a hole for the sling to hang down into when the machine is cocked. It's a bad idea to let the arm jerk a slack sling. Do not set the mangonel on a table or other unstable surface, especially one where you can't secure the mangonel.

The hard way to tune the machine is to adjust the skein. You can either use lots and lots of turns of thinner nylon rope (nylon is the best thing to use, unless you can get a rope made from horse hair!), or add spacer blocks between the sides of the frame and the capstans, effectively making the skein longer. Either of these can improve the power of the machine.

You can also adjust the arm. A lighter weight arm will swing faster, but it will probably also break. A longer arm will have more leverage, but it will also be heavier. We tested a lot of different arms for this kit, and the one we ship it with was the best balance between durability and performance.

Safety:

Please remember that THIS MANGONEL MODEL IS NOT A TOY! It is a representative model of a real ancient military weapon and is intended to be educational. Always use under adult supervision, and be aware that the hook on the end of the arm moves fast enough to rip your skin open, and the arm hits the strike pads hard enough to break bones. NEVER put your fingers or anything else between the arm and the strike beams!

If any part of your machine is damaged or defective, do not fire the machine. Contact us for replacement parts.

This machine is capable of hurling a projectile with enough force to knock someone unconscious, break teeth and bones and rupture eyeballs. You are responsible for your own safety and the safety of others when you demonstrate this machine. PLEASE BE CAREFUL!

The Lithobolos Ballista Plans

We hope you enjoy building and shooting it as much as we've enjoyed creating it. So good luck, and have fun!

Checklist of wooden parts to cut.

2) Skein Frame Beams

2) Skein Frame Braces (with cutouts)

2) Skein Frame Braces (plain)

1) Trough Board

1) Main Beam

2) Winch Plates

1) Winch Rope Anchor

2) Strut mount braces (angle cut)

1) Lateral Brace

2) Main-beam braces with angle cut

1) Tail Prop Beam

1) Strut mount brace

2) Long thin struts

2) Pivot Mount Brackets

1) Pedestal Vertical Post

1) Pedestal Joint Beam

2) Pedestal Base Beams

1) Pedestal Base Cross Beam

4) Pedestal Struts

1) Pivot Mounting Block

2) Arms

4) skein anchor blocks

Dowel Rods

1) 3/4" Winch, 6-1/4" long

2) 1/4" Winch Handles, 2" long

1) 1/2" Pedestal, 6" long

8) 3/8" Skein Frame, 2" long

2) 3/8" Spreader, 2-1/2" long

16) 3/8" Wooden Plugs (optional)

8) 5/16" Skein Anchor blocks, 2" long

2) 5/16" Winch Handle Stop, 2" long

Hardware Checklist:

4) Capstan Bars 3/8" x 3-1/2" steel rod

4) Capstan Plates

17) 1-5/8" Drywall Screws

18) 2" Drywall Screws

1) 42 foot rope (for skein bundles)

1) Pelican Hook Trigger

2) 3/4" Steel Rings

2) Brass Screws small

1) Leather pouch 5" x 2-1/2"

1) 20 foot rope (for trigger, bowstring, etc.)

Tools you will need for asembly:	Tools you will need to cut wood (this is what we used):

1. A clamp capable of spanning 9 inches
2. Phillips head screw driver
   (No. 2 will work for all screws)
3. A small round or half-round file
4. Carpenter's wood glue
5. Sandpaper
6. A carpenter's square
	1. Table saw
	2. Planer to smooth the wood and dimension it to
	   the proper thickness
	3. Miter saw, or chop saw.
	4. Drill press

Material Sources

Many of the materials used in the Ballista can be substituted for with something else. If you have problems locating a specific part, read the instructions concerning that part and use your imagination. Take these plans with you when you visit the hardware store as sometimes a salesperson, once they can see the use of the part, can often suggest a good alternative.

The Capstan Bars are simple steel rods, 3/8" in diameter and 3-1/2" long. These can usually be had at local hardware stores in 3-foot lengths for a few dollars. Some stores will cut them to length for you but you can also cut them yourself with a hacksaw.

The Capstan Plates are large washers, with a 2" outside diameter, 1" inside diameter and about 1/8" thick or a little thicker. Local hardware stores may carry them or you can order them on-line.

Drywall screws, sometimes called Bugle-Head screws, are commonly found at hardware stores and lumber supply stores.

Rope There are several kinds of rope that can be used successfully on the Ballista. We suggest double-braided nylon as it is fairly inexpensive, easy to find, has good weathering and mechanical properties and is easy to work with. For the Skein Bundles and Winch ropes, we suggest a ¼" diameter. For the other ropes used we suggest 1/8" diameters. Ropes of these types can usually be found at local Hardware stores, but there are many on-line sources available on the Internet as well.

Brass Screws are optional but used to secure the Winch Handles to the Winch Dowel (see Fig. 10). The ones we use are 3/8" long. You can also wedge them in place with toothpick tips. If you don't expect to take the Winch apart in the future, you could glue the Winch Handles into the Winch Dowel.

3/4" Steel Rings typically available at most "big box" hardware stores.

Pelican Hook Trigger These are most often found in boating/marine stores, not hardware stores. Here are a few on-line sources:

http://www.reddenmarine.com/   Part number 11461   4" Stainless Steel Pelican Hook

http://www.go2marine.com/index.jsp   Part number 23425   4" Stainless Steel Pelican Hook

http://app.infopia.com/Shop/Control/Product/fp/vpid/2190794/vpcsid/0/SFV/31475
   Part number SDG189780

Leather Pouch 5" x 2-1/2" Leather thickness is usually determined by the weight per square foot, in ounces. For the Ballista Pouch you want a piece of about 8-ounce weight, which is roughly 1/8" thick. You can use other materials as well, such as 2" wide nylon webbing used for seat belts. If there is no leather, craft or hobby shop near you, try looking at other sources, such as the tongue from an old leather shoe, welding gloves, tool bags, etc. There are many sources for leather on the Internet as well.

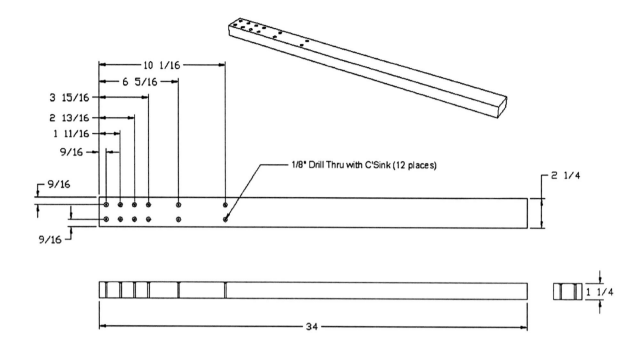

10 1/16
6 5/16
3 15/16
2 13/16
1 11/16
9/16
9/16
9/16
2 1/4

1/8" Drill Thru with C'Sink (12 places)

34

1 1/4

Main Beam (1 each)

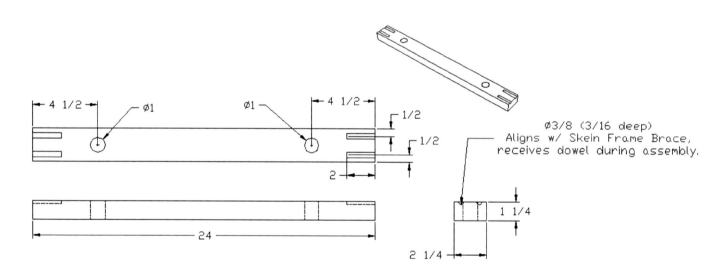

4 1/2
Ø1
Ø1
4 1/2
1/2
1/2
2

24

Ø3/8 (3/16 deep)
Aligns w/ Skein Frame Brace,
receives dowel during assembly.

1 1/4

2 1/4

Skein Frame Beam (2 each)

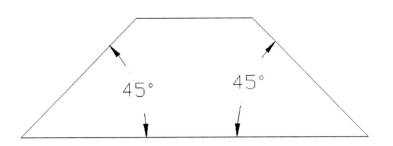

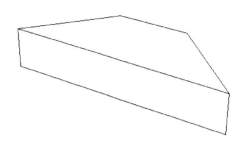

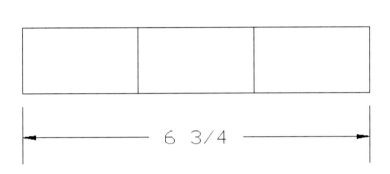

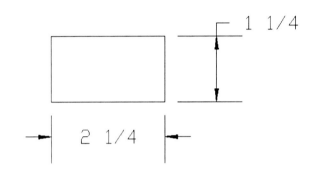

Lateral Brace (1 each)

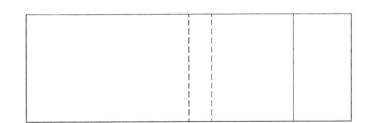

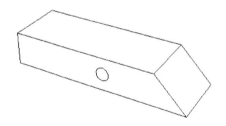

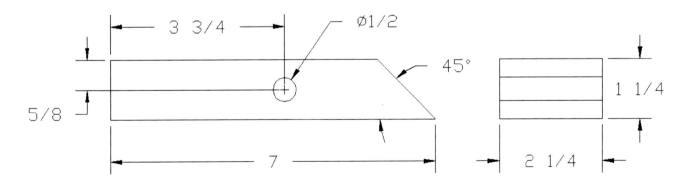

Pedestal Mount Block (1 each)

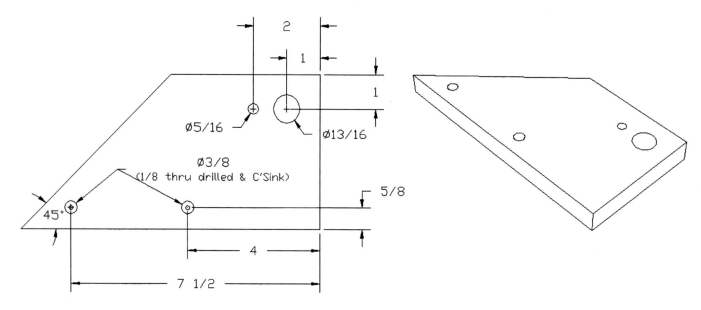

Ø5/16

Ø13/16

Ø3/8
(1/8 thru drilled & C'Sink)

45°

5/8

4

7 1/2

Note: This piece is a mirror image of the "Winch PLate Right". The C'Sink holes are the only difference.

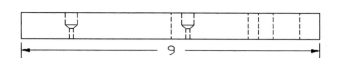

9

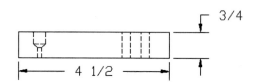

3/4

4 1/2

Winch Plate Left (1 each)

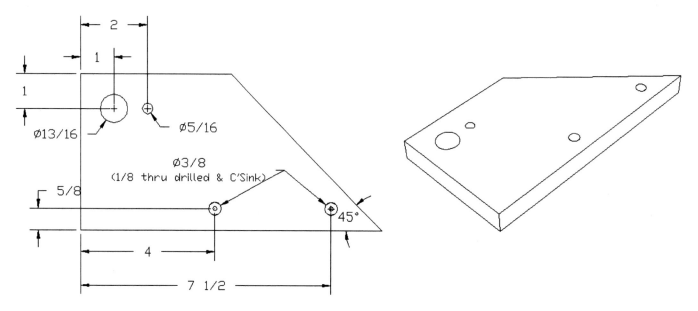

2

1

1

Ø13/16

Ø5/16

Ø3/8
(1/8 thru drilled & C'Sink)

5/8

45°

4

7 1/2

Note: This piece is a mirror image of the "Winch PLate Left". The C'Sink holes are the only difference.

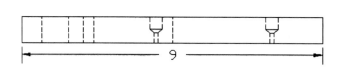

9

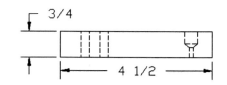

3/4

4 1/2

Winch Plate Right (1 each)

101

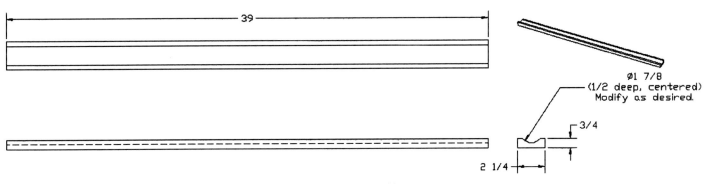

Trough (1 each)

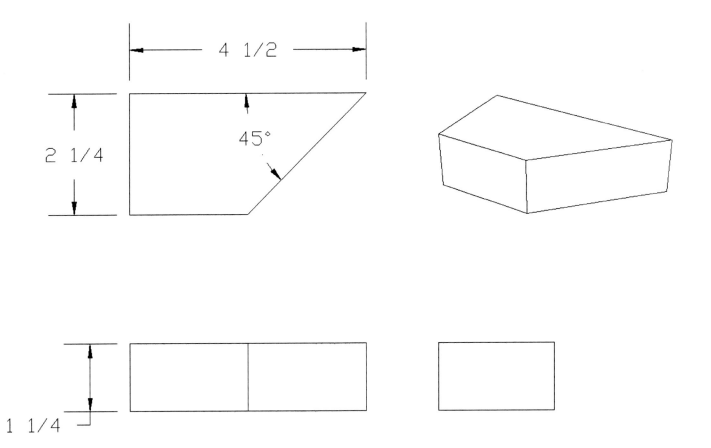

Main Beam Brace (2 each)

102

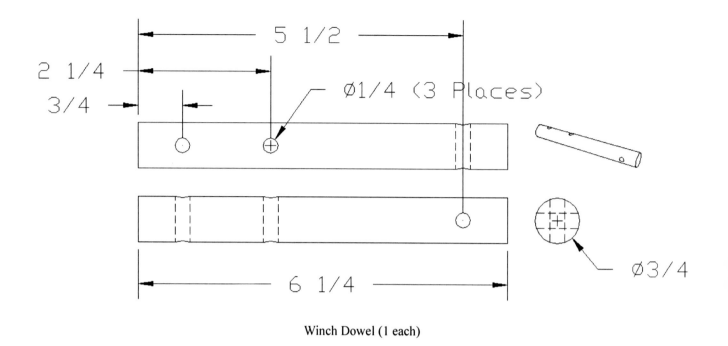

Winch Dowel (1 each)

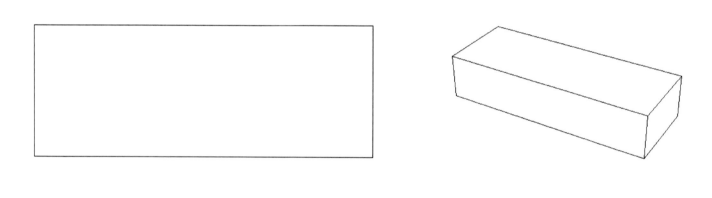

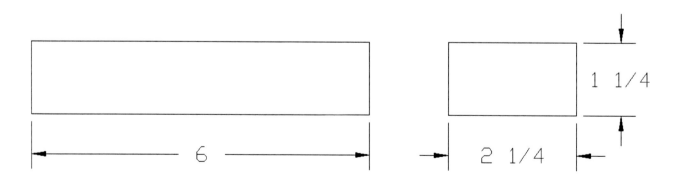

Skein Frame Brace (2 each)

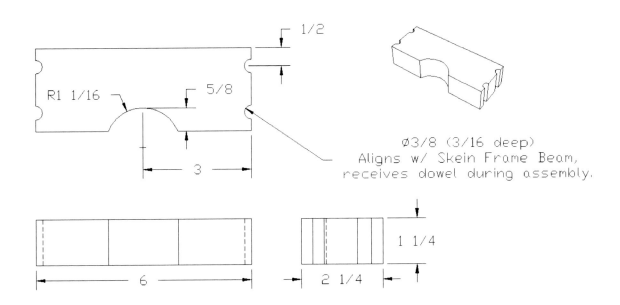

1/2

R1 1/16

5/8

3

Ø3/8 (3/16 deep)
Aligns w/ Skein Frame Beam,
receives dowel during assembly.

6

2 1/4

1 1/4

Skein Frame Brace w/cutout (2 each)

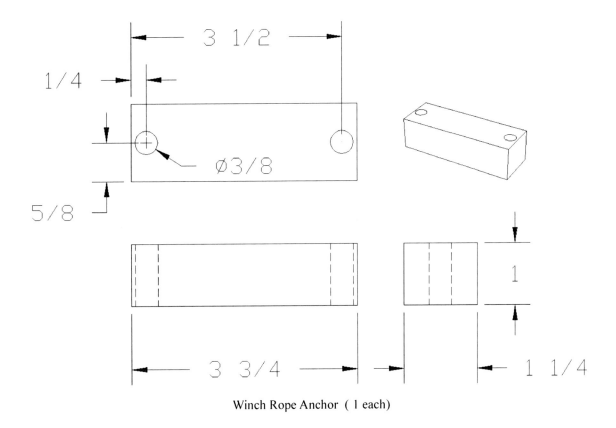

3 1/2

1/4

Ø3/8

5/8

3 3/4

1

1 1/4

Winch Rope Anchor (1 each)

104

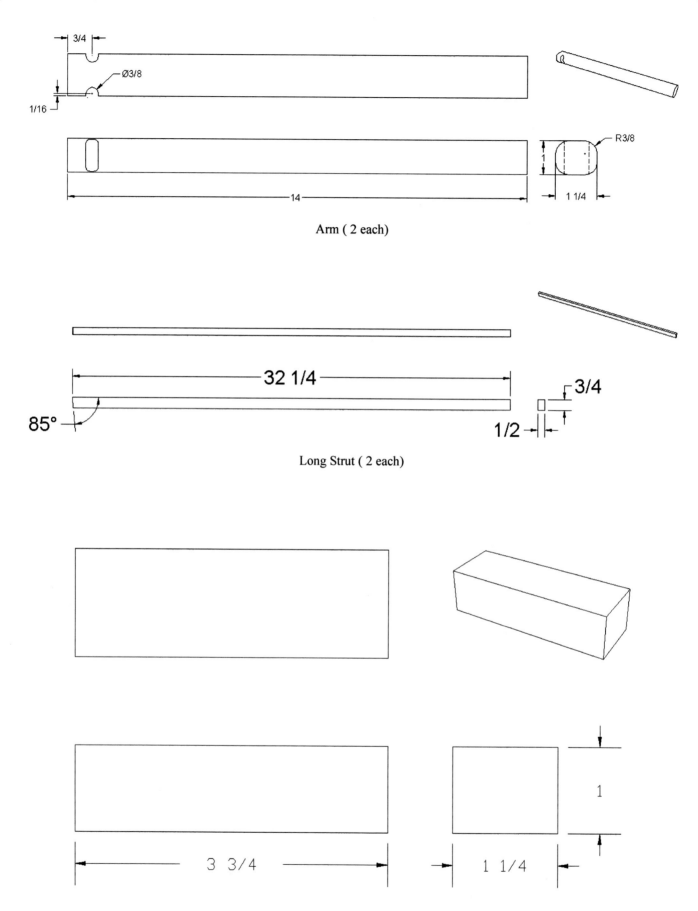

3/4

Ø3/8

1/16

14

R3/8

1

1 1/4

Arm (2 each)

32 1/4

85°

3/4

1/2

Long Strut (2 each)

3 3/4

1 1/4

1

Strut Mount Brace (1 each)

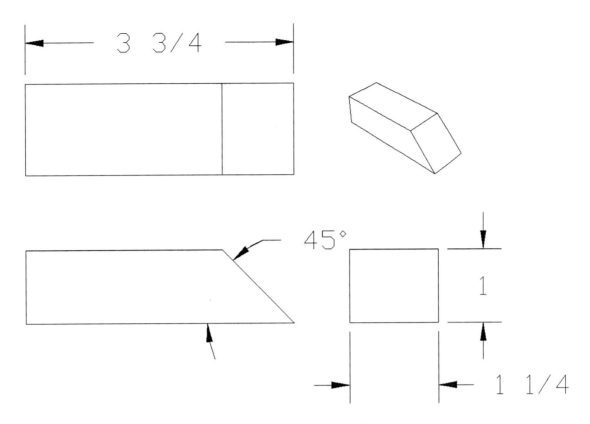

Angled Strut Mount (2 each)

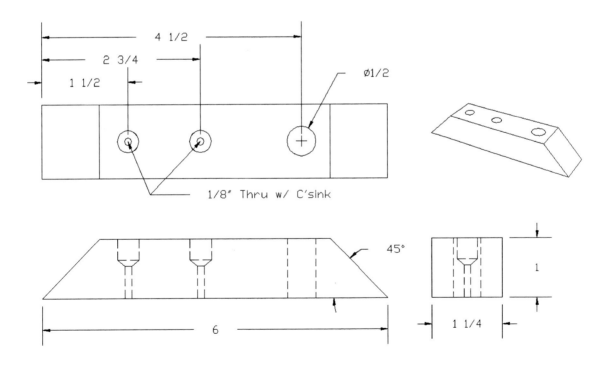

Pivot Mount Bracket (2 each)

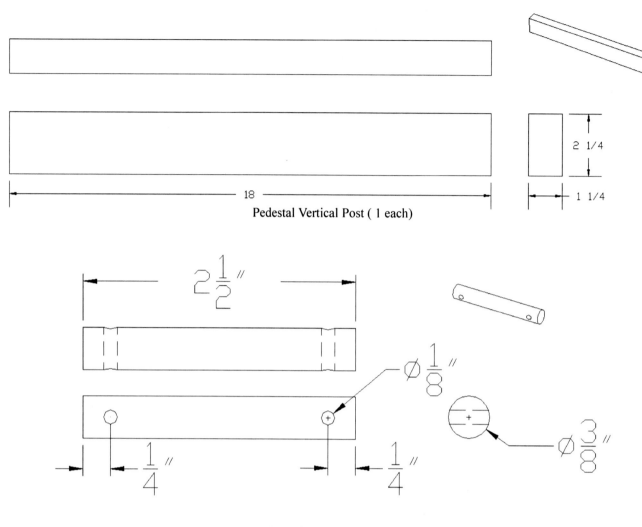

2 1/4

1 1/4

18

Pedestal Vertical Post (1 each)

$2\frac{1}{2}''$

$\varnothing\frac{1}{8}''$

$\frac{1}{4}''$

$\frac{1}{4}''$

$\varnothing\frac{3}{8}''$

Spreader Dowel (2 each)

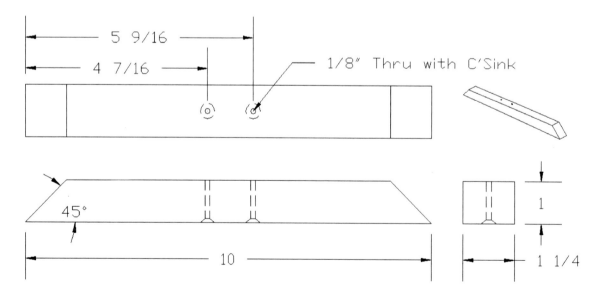

5 9/16

4 7/16

1/8" Thru with C'Sink

45°

1

1 1/4

10

Pedestal Joint Beam (1 each)

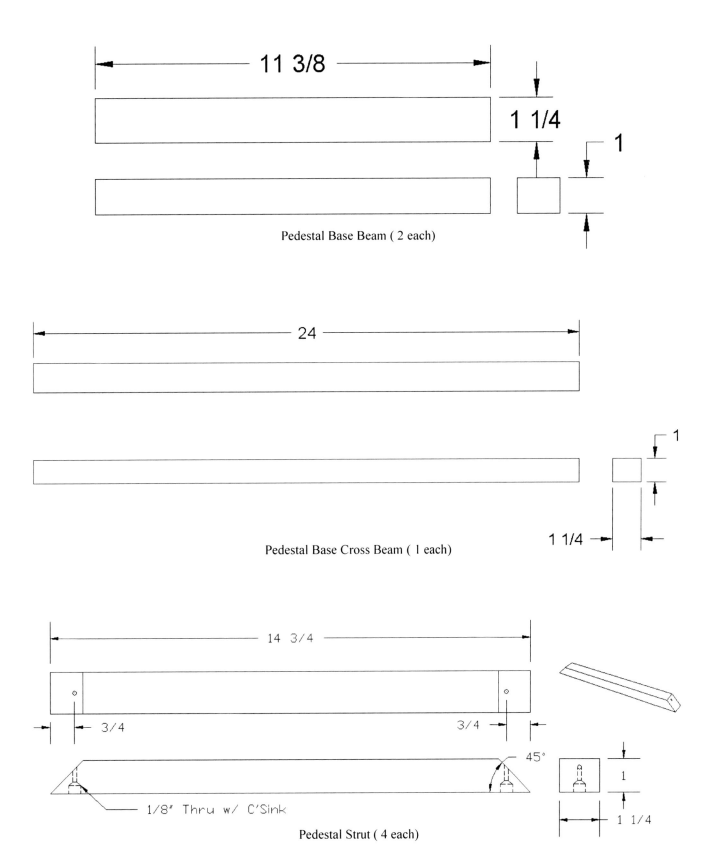

11 3/8

1 1/4

1

Pedestal Base Beam (2 each)

24

1

1 1/4

Pedestal Base Cross Beam (1 each)

14 3/4

3/4

3/4

45°

1

1 1/4

1/8" Thru w/ C'Sink

Pedestal Strut (4 each)

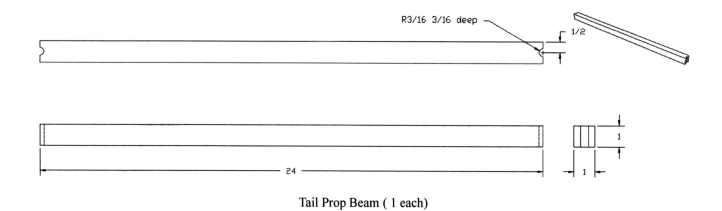

Tail Prop Beam (1 each)

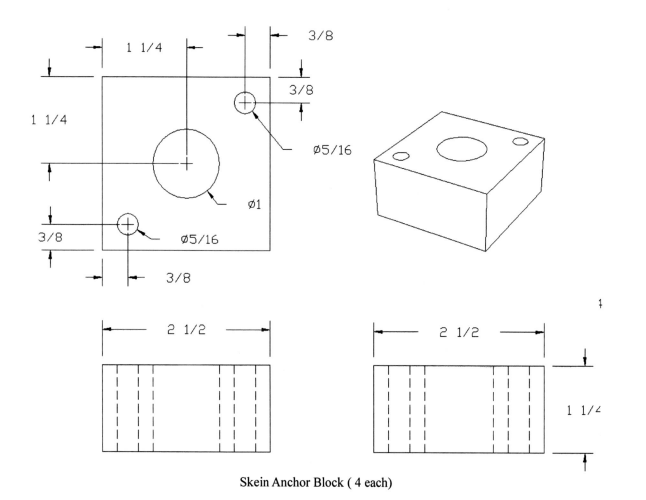

Skein Anchor Block (4 each)

Assembly Instructions

MAIN BEAM
Begin by laying one of the 24" long skein frame pieces on your work surface. The 4 semi-circular groves should be facing up (Fig. 1).

Make a mark in the center of the frame piece, and measure 1-1/8 inches on either side of it. Mark a line at these points, as in Fig. 2. This will be the mounting position for the main beam.

Put a good amount of glue between these marks and place the main beam onto the skein frame beam on the glue, between the marks so that the end of the main beam is flush with the edge of the skein frame beam (Fig. 3). And the angle between the beams is perfectly square (perpendicular).

It's very important that this is a STRONG joint, and that it is square. Clamp the beams in place (but don't cover the screw holes with the clamp!) and check that they are still square and aligned properly. Then drive four of the 2" drywall screws into each of the pre-drilled holes until the heads of the screws sink in flush with the top of the wood. Do this while the glue is still wet for maximum strength. Once all four screws are secure, you can remove the clamp, but don't bump or twist the joint for at least one hour.

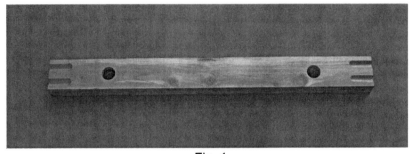

Fig. 1

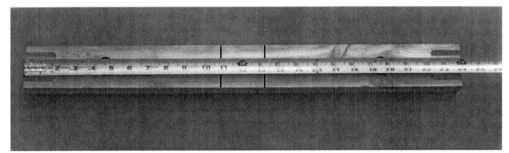

Fig. 2

Fig. 3

Carefully turn the ballista upside down. Glue the lateral brace in place as in Fig. 4. Clamp it in place against the skein frame beam. (Please ignore the 4 extra holes around the large hole!)

Carefully turn the ballista back over, and drive four 2" drywall screws in to the holes to attach the main beam to the lateral brace until the heads of the screws sink in flush with the wood (Fig. 5). Be careful not to disturb the clamp on the skein frame beam. Leave the clamp on until the glue has set.

Fig. 4

Fig. 5

The next piece is the pedestal mount block. Screw it into place using four 2" drywall screws just like the last piece (Fig. 6). Gluing is not necessary, but it's not a bad idea either. Fig. 6 also shows an alternate way to clamp the lateral brace.

The trough board will cover up all those screw heads, so make sure they are all sunk in flush with the wood, or sunk into the wood a little.

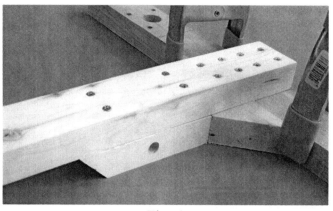
Fig. 6

WINCH ASSEMBLY

The two winch plates are mirror images of each other. They must be installed with the large countersink hole to the outside, so the wooden peg can hide the screw head. Make a mark 3 inches from the flat end of the winch plate, on the inside of the plate (Fig. 7)

Screw the plate to the main beam (Fig. 8) so that it is flush with the bottom of the main beam. Insert the winch dowel to insure proper alignment with the other plate, and screw the second plate onto the main beam too (Fig. 9).

Attach the winch anchor to the back of the winch plates as in Fig. 10. Now put wooden plugs into all six of the screw holes to cover up the screw heads. You may need to tap them in with a rubber or wooden mallet (or tap lightly with a hammer). If any of them are loose, you may want to use a drop of glue to hold them in place.

With the winch dowel in place, slide a ¾" steel ring over each end, and then insert the winch handles (¼" dowel pins) into the holes near the ends of the winch dowel (Fig 10). The rings will prevent the winch handles from rubbing against the sides of the plates. Secure the winch handles with a small brass screw in the large dowel as in Fig 10.

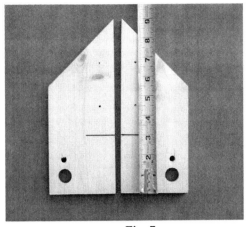

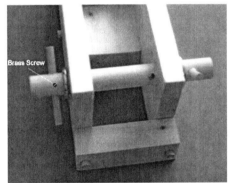

Fig. 7   Fig. 8

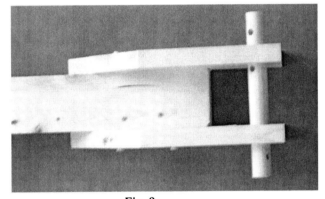

Fig. 9   Fig 10

TROUGH BOARD

Make a mark 2 ½ inches from the end of the main beam and glue the trough board onto the main beam at this mark (Fig. 11). The second board should protrude beyond the front of the skein frame several inches.

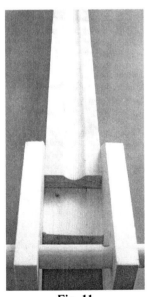

Fig. 11   Fig. 12

THE SKEIN FRAME

On the bottom frame beam (it's already attached to the main beam), place a drop of glue into each of the four groves, and put one of the 3/8" x 2" wooden dowels into each groove (Fig. 13). Then glue the main-beam braces on either side of the main beam (Figs. 14, 15, 16.)

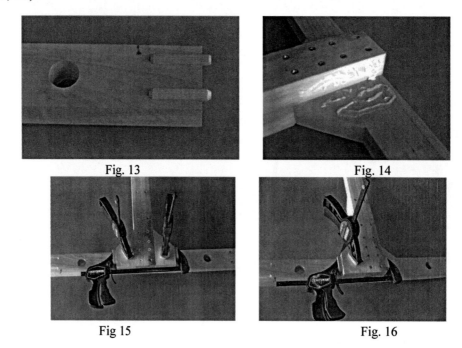

Fig. 13   Fig. 14

Fig 15   Fig. 16

Glue the plain skein-frame braces to the skein frame against the braces you just glued into place. Fig. 17. Then glue the cut-out braces on the ends, as in Figs. 18, 19.

Fig 17   Fig 18

Try the fit of the brace blocks on the round posts. Be sure you have the orientation of the cut-outs toward the inside of the frame (Fig 19). You may need to file the grooves a little for a snug, flush fit (Fig 20). Glue the brace in place as in Fig. 19.

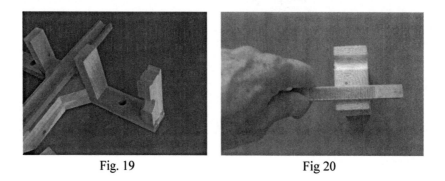

Fig. 19   Fig 20

Once all four braces are in place, glue the other frame beam on top of this assembly (Fig. 21). Make sure that all joints are square (true 90 degree angles). If you don't have any clamps capable of holding the top frame piece on, use a heavy weight like we did in Fig. 21.

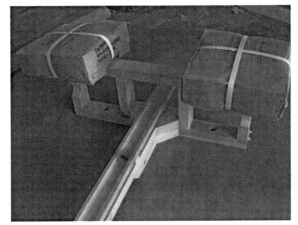
Fig. 21.

The frame brace struts are simply glued into place. Start by gluing the 3 ¾" block in the center-back of the top frame piece, as in Fig 22. After the glue dries, glue the first strut into place and clamp it at both ends, Figs 23 and 24. Do the same thing to the other side, and then glue the strut end-pieces into place (Fig. 25.)
The holes in the struts should go in the back, at the winch plates. You can put a wooden plug in the hole to give the appearance of being attached with a fastener.

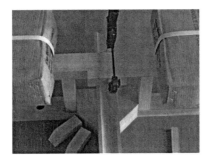
Fig. 22

Fig. 23

Fig 24

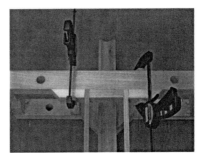
Fig 25.

114

THE SKEINS

First, cut the 42-foot rope into 2 pieces, each 21 feet long. Be sure to fuse the ends.

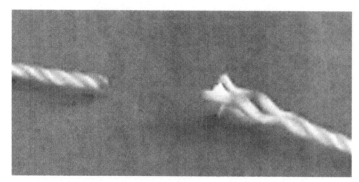

Fig. 26

Fusing is a technique used on nylon and poly ropes to melt the end of the rope and prevent it from unraveling. You can even melt the end into a small button making it almost impossible to slip through a knot. In the photo (Fig. 26), the end on the right is not fused, but the one on the left is. Do this by holding the end near a small flame or heat source just until it begins to melt. But don't catch the rope on fire!

Use one 21 foot long piece of rope for each skein.
The skein is the source of power for your machine. The more powerful you want your machine to be, the longer it will take to build the skein. For easy construction and a machine that can throw golf balls about 75 to 100 feet, use 5 loops on the skein (5 strands on one side of the arm, and 5 on the other). To shoot a golf ball 150 to 200 feet, we used 11 wraps on our model. The more wraps you use, the harder it will be to tension the skein, and the harder it will be to cock the machine when firing. Using too much tension will damage the machine so don't go crazy!

Note: In some of the pictures that follow, the skein anchor blocks are not shown. (We didn't have time for all new photography before taking the instructions to the printer, so some of them are of an older model). Be sure to put the skein anchor plates (Fig 27) on the top and bottom of your skein frame so that the completed skein will look like Fig. 28 when you're done.

Fig 27

Fig 28

Put the capstan plates (large metal rings) over the holes on the skein anchors outside of the frame (Fig. 29), and lay the capstan bars over these plates centered over the holes. Using clamps to hold everything in place will make this easier (Fig. 30).

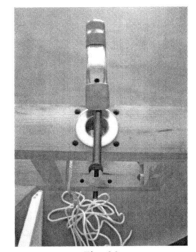

Fig. 29   Fig. 30

Tie (or clamp) one end of the polyester rope to the bottom of the frame, and pass it up through the skein hole. Thread it around the capstans, keeping the bundle neat, as in Fig 31. After you get one or two wraps in, put the arm in the bundle so that it keeps the two sides of the bundle separate (Fig. 31).

Fig. 31   Fig. 32

Once you've got four or five wraps in, it's ok if the new wraps overlap the previous ones. Just make sure they don't cross over in the middle. If you're having trouble getting the rope past the other loops and through the holes, a large crochet needle will help, or you can make a loop from a clothes hanger or other stiff wire to help pull through the rope ends through the holes.

Once you've got all your loops in place, untie the rope from the frame and tie the ends of the rope together in a secure square knot over the capstan (Fig. 32). Fuse the ends into a button so it won't slip. Position the arm up so its bottom end extends past the skein about 1 inch (Fig 28).
Do the same thing to the other skein. Make sure that they both have the same number of wraps, and they are equally tight. Too much slack in one skein can cause it to be unbalanced.

Use a large wrench, or we like to use a 6" C-clamp to tighten the skein anchor plates. Be sure to turn them away from the main beams, in the direction you want the arm to move (Fig. 33). Do this for the top and the bottom of the skein equally. The arm should swing into place when you do this. Make only a ¼ turn on each side at a time, then do the other side. Otherwise the arm will not stay centered in the skein.

116

Your completed skeins should look something like Fig. 34. (We used nine loops in this photo)

Fig 33   Fig 34

How many turns to use will depend on how many loops you have and how much tension (if any) is already in the skein. At least one full twist is usually enough, but you can use more if you want to. It should be hard to turn. The harder it is to turn, the more force you are storing in the twist. You may be wondering, "What prevents the skein anchor plates from untwisting?" Friction is the answer. The skeins are actually pulling the plates inward (into the frame) with much more force than they are twisting the plates. We made over a dozen of these in our testing, and only one has slipped.

If your skein anchor slips, we do not recommend gluing or screwing them into place. You'll want to re-tension your skeins from time to time as the rope relaxes. Eventually you won't need to re-tension them anymore, but for the first few weeks you will. If your anchor block slips, get a piece of twine and tie it to the frame (Fig 30), then strap it TIGHTLY around the anchor block (Fig. 31) in the direction of the slipping. This will hold it in place. If the skeins are tight, the block should press into the frame beam over time so that you should be able to remove the strapping and the block should stay in place. Changes in temperature, humidity and even atmospheric pressure can affect the skeins and the anchor blocks.

Fig 35   Fig 36

Ballista Bow String Assembly

The Ballista Throwing Arms should be mounted in the skeins of rope but the skeins do not have to be at full tension, just enough to hold the Throwing Arms in place is sufficient. During the first stages of constructing the Bow String, we are simply mounting it, along with the Spreaders, Pouch and Bridle Loops. Once assembled, all the pieces will be "touched up" for final positioning and the Bow String tension adjusted. This may seem overly complex but the results are well worth the effort!

117

From the 20-foot rope cut 2 lengths at 12" long each, these will become the two Pouch Bridle Loops. Cut 1 length at 8 feet long, this will become the main Bow String. Fuse all cut ends, by the same method mentioned elsewhere in these instructions.

We'll be starting with the 8 foot long piece, which is longer than needed but gives extra length to assemble the Bow String, it's easier to work with a longer piece at this point and the excess length can be cut off later.

1) Start with a simple loop knotted in one end of the Bow String and tightened. This loop only needs to be about 1 inch in length. (Fig 37)

2) About 5 inches from that knot, make a double-loop and slip it on to one end of either Throwing Arm. Leave the 1 inch loop dangle for now.

3) 9 inches along the longer piece of the string, make a Clover Hitch. (Fig 39) This goes over the end of one of the Separator dowels. The smaller dowel is then inserted between the two turns of the Clover Hitch and through that end of the Separator dowel.

4) Now thread the string through the four holes in one end of the Pouch, either the upper or lower edge seen in Fig 40.

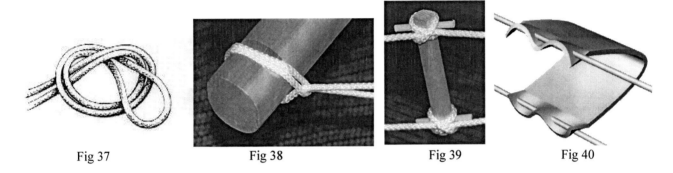

| Fig 37 | Fig 38 | Fig 39 | Fig 40 |

5) Make a second Clover Hitch and place it over one end of the second Separator Dowel. Keep the spacing about the same as between the Pouch and the first Separator Dowel. They can be adjusted for final positioning later.

6) Make a second double-loop (Fig 38) and place it over the end of the second Throwing Arm. Adjust the Bow string, by feeding it through the double-loop, to keep most of the slack out.

7) Now another Clover Hitch on the bottom of the second Separator Dowel, through the other four holes in the Pouch, and a final Clover Hitch on the first Separator Dowel.

8) Thread the loose end of the Bow String through the loop that was left dangling in the beginning and make a Taught-line hitch (Fig 41). Don't tighten the knot next to the loop, but an inch or so away from it. A Taught-line hitch can be used to tighten or loosen the Bow String without having to be untied! Fig 41 shows the Taught-line hitch 'loose', as if just tied but not tightened down yet, for clarity. Once you've tied the knot, tighten it down.

Fig 41

9) Now for the Bridle-loops. One will be tied to the upper Bow String, in two places, and the other to the lower Bow String, again in two places. Use a Bowline knot for these and place the knots about 1" to 1-1/2" away from either side of the Pouch. (Fig 42)

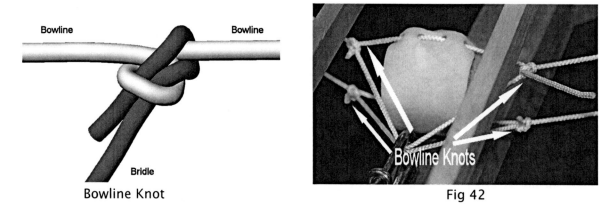

Bowline Knot

Fig 42

The Bow String is designed such that it can be modified easily, by hand in just a couple of minutes, to accommodate desired changes in the Bow String tension or Payload size. The overall length of the string, position of the string separators, Pouch and Pouch Bridle loops, and length of Bridle loops, can all be changed.

THE PEDESTAL

Start with the base of the pedestal. Center the joint beam on the bottom of the vertical post as in Fig. 43 and use two of the 1-5/8" drywall screws to attach it. Center the cross beam on the joint beam so that it is perpendicular (Fig 45). Attach it with a 2" drywall screw. Attach the two base beams to the joint beam with the 1-5/8" drywall screws so that they are tightly against the crossbeam (Figs 46, 47). Stand the pedestal up on its base and insure that all joints are a true 90 degrees (Fig 48).

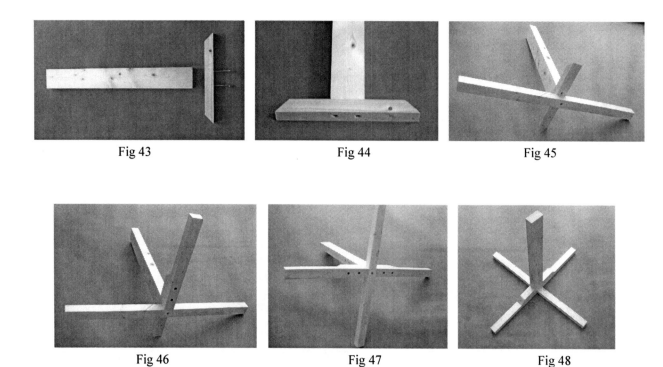

Fig 43   Fig 44   Fig 45

Fig 46   Fig 47   Fig 48

Now attach the four struts using the 1-5/8" drywall screws as in Fig 49.

Get the two mounting brackets and make a mark 2 ¾" from the end with the large hole, on the inside of the piece. Put glue on one of the mount brackets below the line and attach it to the side of the vertical support with the 1-5/8" drywall screws as in Fig 50. Use the ½" pedestal dowel to insure a proper alignment, and glue and screw the other mount bracket onto the support (Fig. 51).

  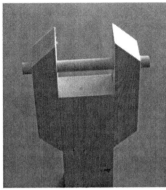

| Fig 49 | Fig 50 | Fig 51 |

Insert wooden plugs into all the holes. Mount the ballista frame on the pedestal. Use the tail prop piece to hold up the tail of the machine. The grooves in each end of the tail prop fit onto the corner of the pedestal base and on the winch rope anchor piece.

THE TRIGGER, COCKING, LOADING AND FIRING

With the bowstring mounted, open the trigger and attach it behind the pouch to both Bridle loops, as in Fig. 52. Tie the 4-foot length of rope to the pull-ring. This is the trigger release line.

| Fig 52 | Fig 54 | Fig. 55 |

With the 5-foot length of rope, tie one end to the winch anchor block, thread the other end through the bottom eye of the trigger, and back to the winch dowel. Insert the loose end into the winch dowel hole and pull it to take-up the slack in the line. Tie a knot in the end of the line to prevent it from slipping back through the winch dowel hole, cut the excess off and fuse the end (or you can melt the end of the rope into a button shape instead of knotting it). (Fig. 55).

Fig 54 is the view from the front of the machine, with old Bow String design. To cock the machine, turn the winch handles until the trigger is all the way back, then put a wooden peg into the hole to prevent the winch from unwinding.

Once the machine is cocked, carefully place a golf ball in the trough, with the leather pouch snugly behind it. To fire the machine, stand at least three feet behind it and pull the trigger release cord!

SAFETY AND TROUBLESHOOTING

Keep in mind that this is not a toy! It is a working model of a real ancient military weapon. Always treat it with respect, just like you would with any weapon. Never fire a machine that is damaged or improperly constructed. Always be sure that there are no people and no property for at least 300 feet in front of the machine, and 50 feet to either side.

The Petraria Arcatinus Catapult Plans

Hardware Required:

4 wooden dowels 1/4 inch diameter 2" long	**20 feet of twine**	**10 wood screws** Size #6 2-1/4" long
4 wooden dowels 5/16 inch dia., 2-1/2" long	**3 eye screws** 1/4" eye diameter 1/2" shank length.	**2 square hooks:** A = 1-3/8" long B = 1/2" long
6 wooden plugs 3/8" dia.	**6 washers** 5/16" inside diameter.	**1 strip of leather** 1" wide by 8" long. 1/8" thick, or thicker.

Other Hardware:
1 steel bow – 50 lb. replacement bow for pistol crossbows are what we use. These can be found easily on-line, most gun shops, some knife shops, and many sporting goods stores carry them as well – usually for under $10. They come in fiberglass and steel varieties. We prefer the steel bows.
Be sure to get the bowstring and endcaps to go with it too.

Wooden parts (see drawings at end):
2 side rails 18 inches long x 2-1/4"
2 foot beams, 7-3/4 inches long
1 winch dowel
2 winch posts with a ¾ inch hole
1 main floor beam 16" long
2 long struts, 15-3/4" long, angled ends
1 winch hook bar, 3-1/2" long
1 trigger, 3-1/8" x ¾" x ¾"
1 main spar, 10 inches long, funky.
1 bow anchor plate
4 wheels

1 trigger prop (smallest piece)
1 trigger handle 9-1/4 inches long
1 trigger handle mount 2-1/4 inches long
2 arm mount plates 3" x 3" x ¾"
2 spoon mounts (small parallelogram)
2 spoon sides 3-1/2 inches long
1 spoon end 1-3/4 inches long
1 arm strike bar
2 short struts, 6-1/2" long, angled ends
2 wheel axles
1 arm, rounded on one side.

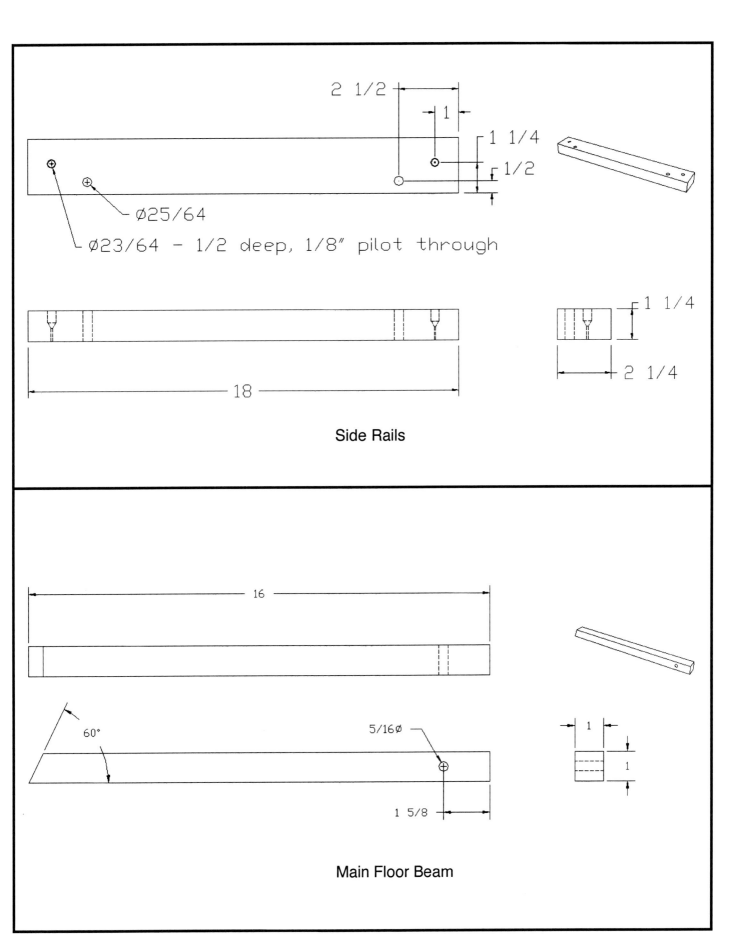

2 1/2

1

1 1/4

1/2

Ø25/64

Ø23/64 − 1/2 deep, 1/8″ pilot through

1 1/4

2 1/4

18

Side Rails

16

60°

5/16Ø

1 5/8

1

1

Main Floor Beam

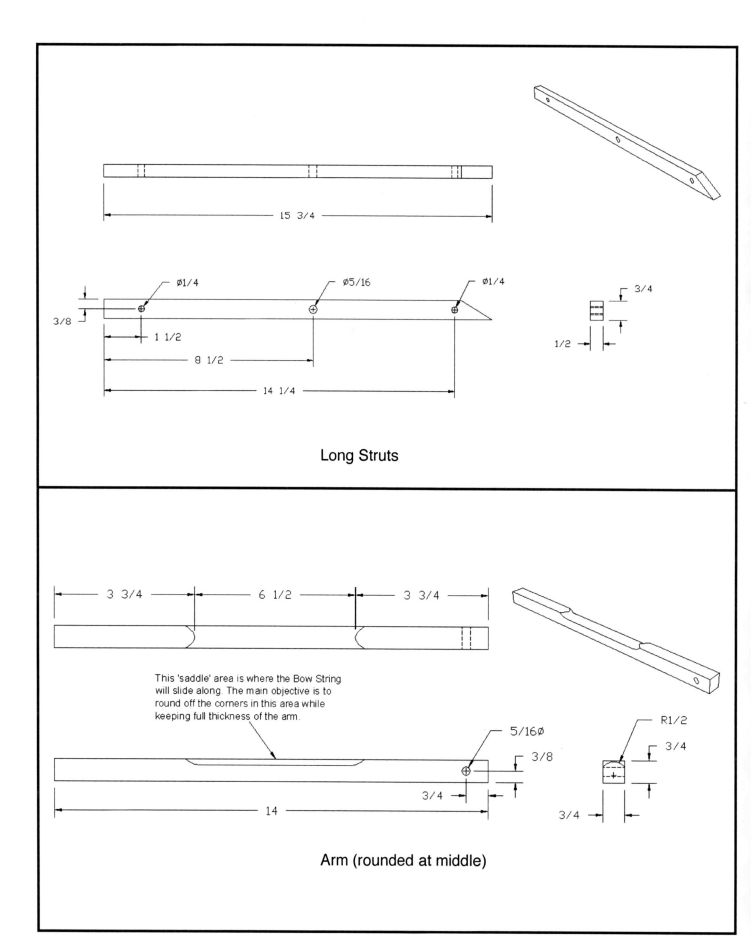

15 3/4

Ø1/4   Ø5/16   Ø1/4

3/4

3/8

1/2

1 1/2

8 1/2

14 1/4

Long Struts

3 3/4   6 1/2   3 3/4

This 'saddle' area is where the Bow String
will slide along. The main objective is to
round off the corners in this area while
keeping full thickness of the arm.

5/16Ø

R1/2

3/8

3/4

14

3/4

3/4

Arm (rounded at middle)

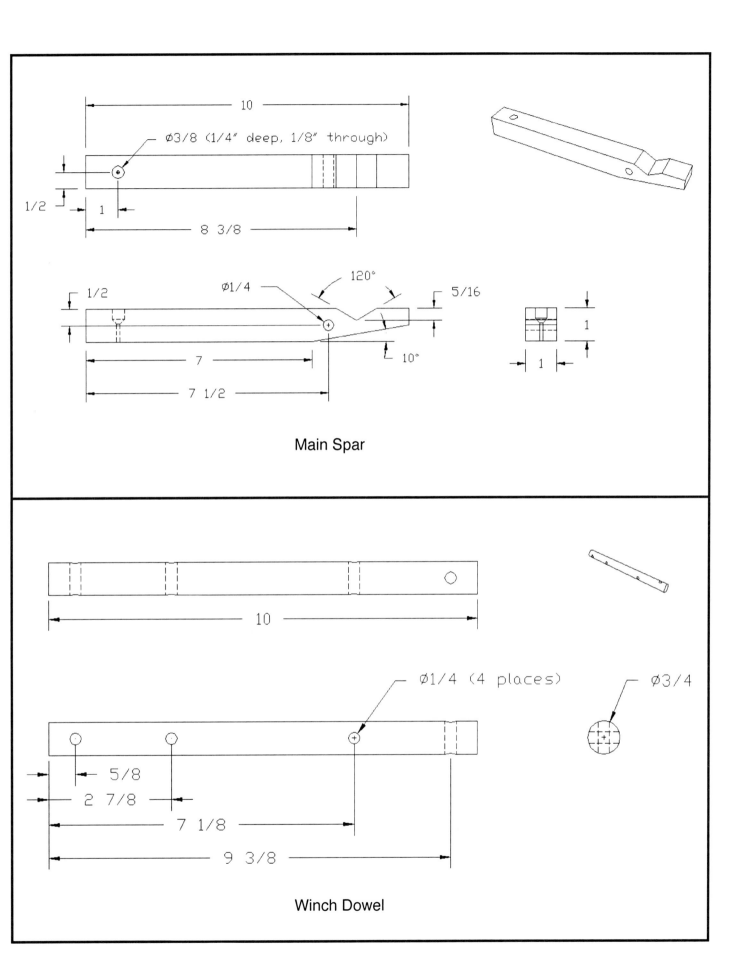

Ø3/8 (1/4" deep, 1/8" through)

10

1/2

1

8 3/8

1/2

Ø1/4

120°

5/16

1

7

7 1/2

10°

1

Main Spar

10

Ø1/4 (4 places)

Ø3/4

5/8

2 7/8

7 1/8

9 3/8

Winch Dowel

124

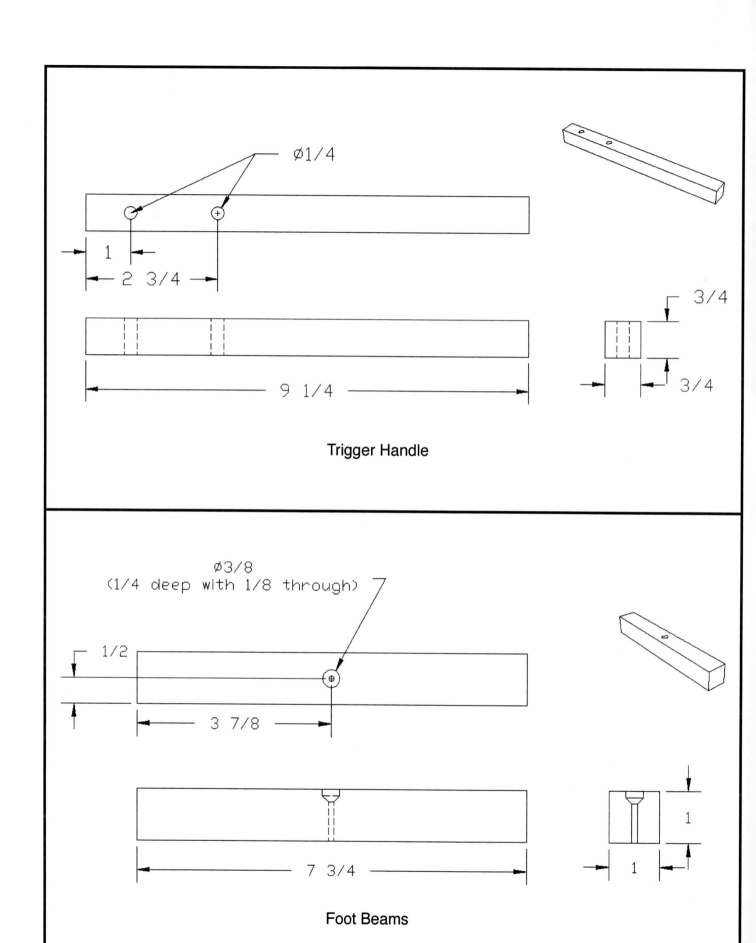

Ø1/4

1

2 3/4

9 1/4

3/4

3/4

Trigger Handle

Ø3/8
(1/4 deep with 1/8 through)

1/2

3 7/8

7 3/4

1

1

Foot Beams

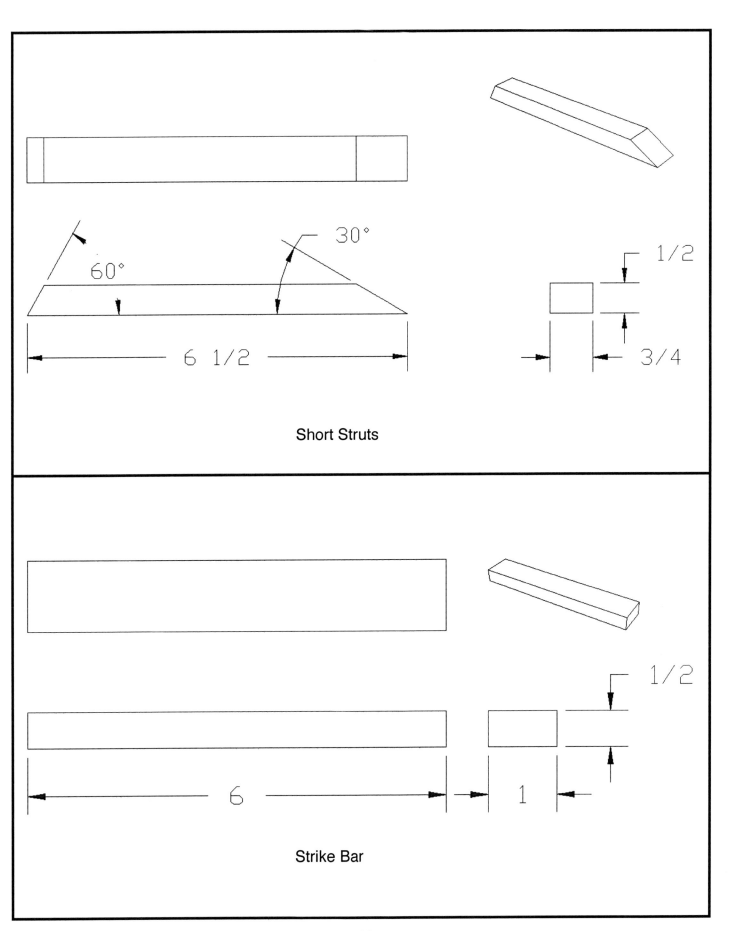

Short Struts

60°

30°

6 1/2

1/2

3/4

Strike Bar

1/2

6

1

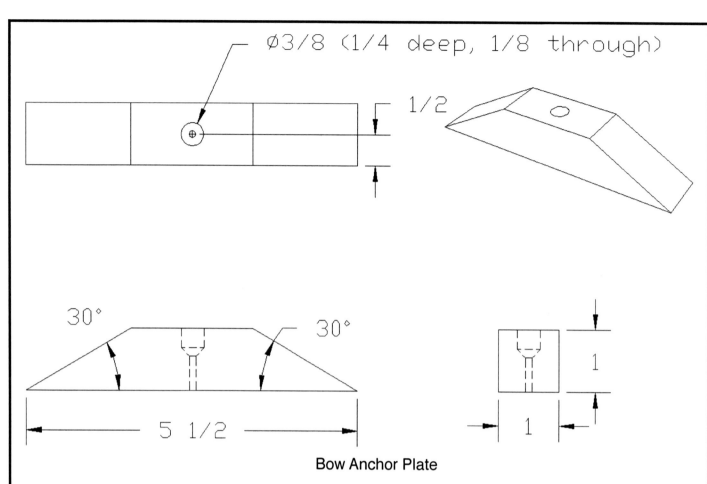

Ø3/8 (1/4 deep, 1/8 through)

1/2

30°   30°

5 1/2

1

1

Bow Anchor Plate

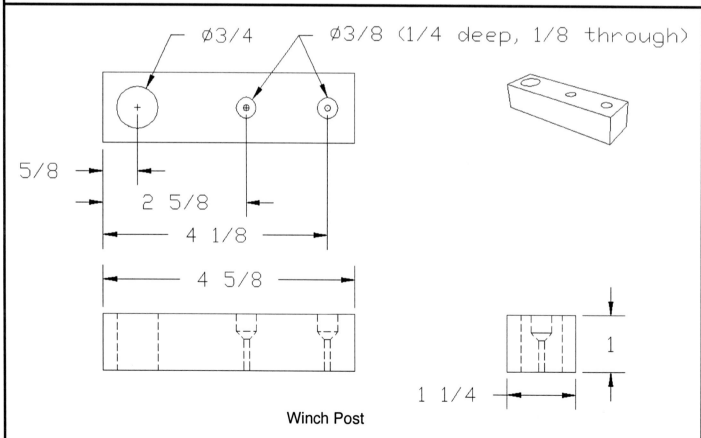

Ø3/4   Ø3/8 (1/4 deep, 1/8 through)

5/8

2 5/8

4 1/8

4 5/8

1

1 1/4

Winch Post

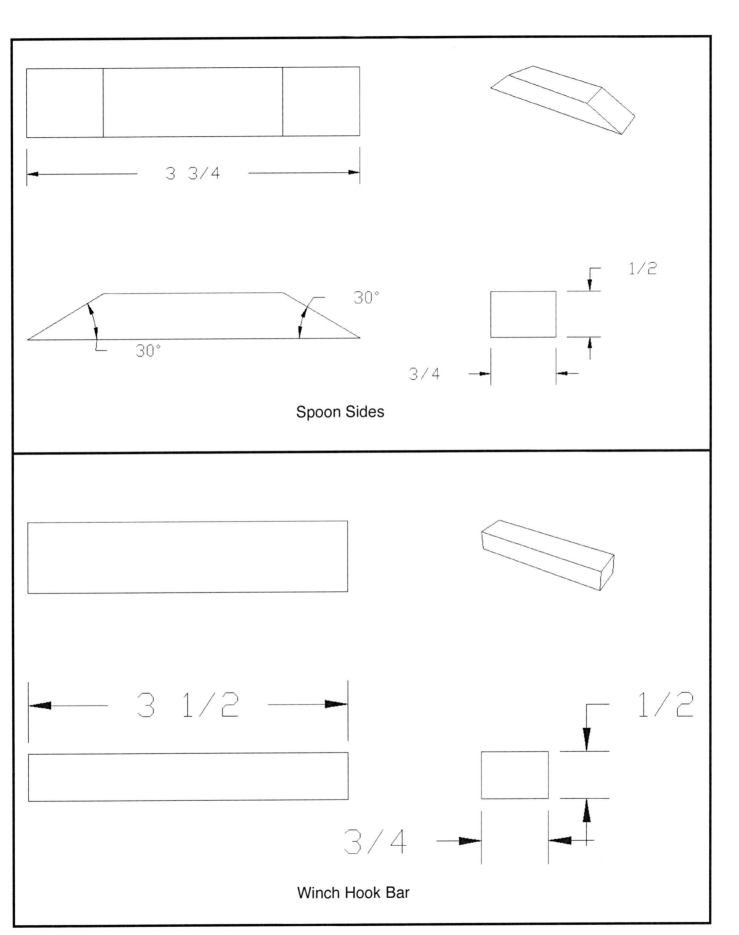

3 3/4

30°

30°

1/2

3/4

Spoon Sides

3 1/2

1/2

3/4

Winch Hook Bar

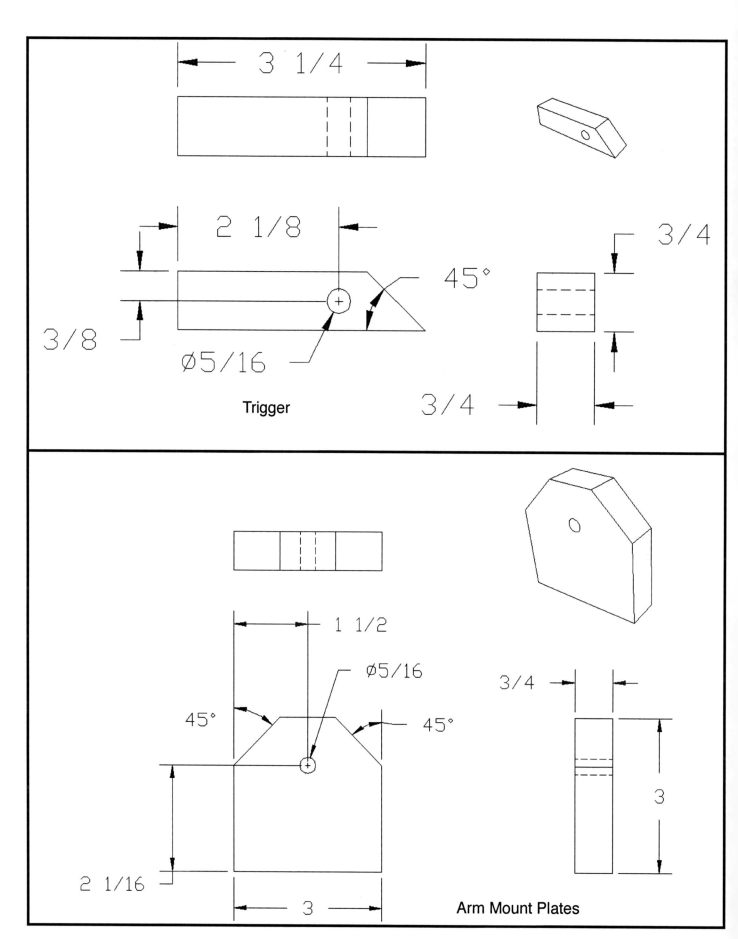

3 1/4

2 1/8

3/4

45°

3/8

Ø5/16

Trigger

3/4

1 1/2

Ø5/16

45°

45°

3/4

3

2 1/16

3

Arm Mount Plates

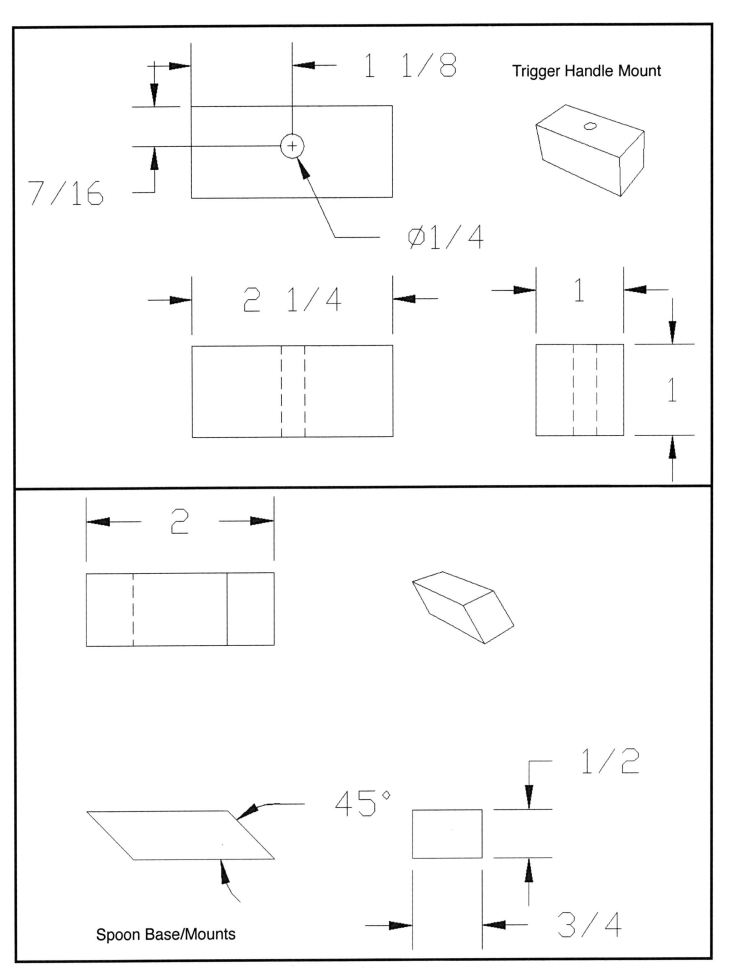

1 1/8

Trigger Handle Mount

7/16

Ø1/4

2 1/4

1

1

2

45°

1/2

3/4

Spoon Base/Mounts

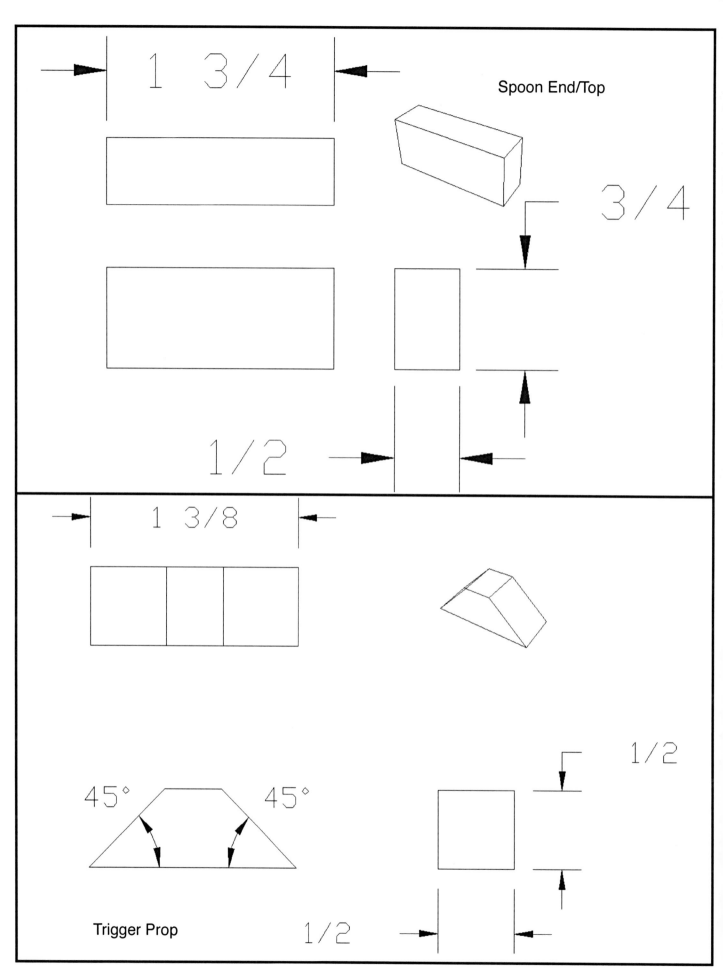

1 3/4

Spoon End/Top

3/4

1/2

1 3/8

45°   45°

Trigger Prop

1/2

1/2

1/2

Assembly Instructions:
1. The main triangle.

The main triangle is made from the spar beam, the base beam, and the two long struts.

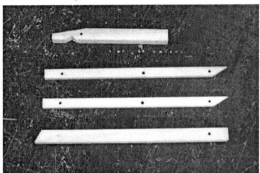

Fig. 1

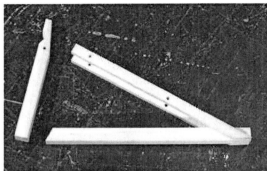

Fig. 2

Attach the angled end of the long struts to the base beam using a 5/16" dowel. DO NOT GLUE. You'll need to take one of these off again later. Then attach the main spar to the struts with another 5/16" dowel. Again, do not glue. Make sure the main spar is flush with the bottom of the base beam, and screw it together with one of the wood screws (fig. 4).

Fig. 3

Fig. 4

This might be a good time to glue a few things that we'll need later. Get the piece of leather and the strike block, and glue the leather to the block so that it curves around both the top and the bottom (Fig. 5). Glue the trigger prop onto the trigger piece as in fig. 6.

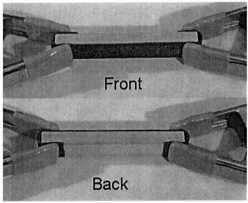

Front

Back

Fig. 5

Fig. 6

Now screw two "feet" onto the bottom of the main triangle. It is very important that these feet are centered You may find this easier to do by turning the triangle upside down and making a mark on the end of the main spar as in fig. 7. The tip of the screw should go into the crossed lines. The other "foot" should be flush with the end of the main beam. Once you're got the legs screwed on, turn the triangle right-side up (fig 10).

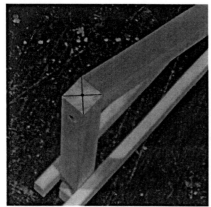

Fig. 7

Fig. 8

Fig. 9

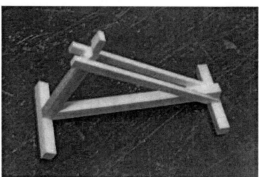

Fig. 10

Glue the strike pad onto the angled portion of the main spar as in fig. 11. We'll use the trigger later. The main triangle is now complete.

Fig. 11

2. The Arm, Winch and Trigger

Get the arm and two mount blocks, two of the washers and a 5/16" dowel. Assemble them together as in fig. 13, with one washer on each side of the arm, in between the mount plates. The rounded side of the arm should be towards the bottom.

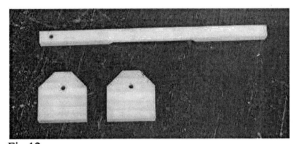

Fig 12

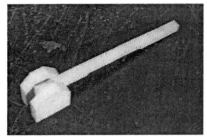

Fig. 13

Put this assembly inside the main triangle so that the flat side of the arm is flat against the strike pad, and the mount plates straddle the main base beam, as in fig. 14. Use a clamp to hold the arm in place while you adjust the plates. They should be flush with the bottom of the main base beam.

Fig. 14

Fig. 15

Fig. 16

Glue the mount plates to the main base beam with a good wood glue. Be sure to clamp it in place while the glue dries. Once you've got one clamp set, you can remove the clamp holding the arm and use it for the mount plates too (figs. 15, 16.) While that dries, we'll start work on the side rails.

Get the two side rails and the two winch mount bars. Lay the side rails so that the bottoms (the edge near the two holes) are together, as in fig. 17. Screw the winch mount bars onto the side rails so that they are flush with the bottom and also flush with one of the holes. Make sure they are square and that an axle can still pass thorough the hole, but don't leave any space between the hole and the mounts! See fig. 18.

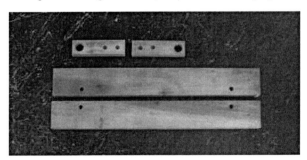

Fig 17

Fig 18

If the glue on your arm mount plates is completely dry now, we can attach the side rails to the main body. Line them up as in fig. 19, with the winch mount bars on the inside and near the rear of the machine. Screw the rear foot beams to the side rails so that there is exactly ½ inch of space from the top of the side rail to the top of the foot beam, and ¼ inch of space from the rear of the foot beam to the end of the side rail, as in fig. 20. The screw holes won't line up with the center of the beam, but that's ok. Put the winch dowel into the holes to make sure it turns properly. The winch dowel should barely touch the struts.

Fig. 19

Fig. 20

You might need to take one of the struts off for this step. The trigger should be installed between the struts so that the prop block faces the front of the machine. Put two washers on each side of the trigger. Then put the long strut back on the machine.

Fig 21

Assemble the trigger handle onto the trigger handle mount as in fig. 23. Don't glue anything, just put the ¼" dowels in the holes.

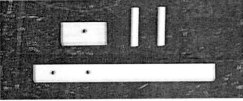

Fig. 22

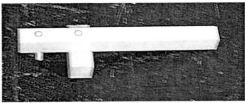

Fig 23

You're going to glue the mount block onto the side of the main floor beam as in fig. 24, but alignment is critical, so first put the whole trigger handle assembly on the frame so the mount block is on one side and the dowel is on the other side. Use a clamp to hold the mount block in place while you align it.

Move it as necessary to make the rear edge of the trigger handle line-up with the bottom corner of the trigger, when the trigger handle is perpendicular (90 degrees) to the floor beam, as in fig. 25. The mount block should also be flush with the top and bottom of the beam. Then make a small mark with a pencil on the floor beam at either end of the block. Remove the trigger handle and glue the trigger mount block in place, according to your marks, as in fig. 24. When the glue is dry, reinstall the handle.

Fig. 24

Fig 25

Now that all that's done, the long struts MUST be glued securely to the sides of the main spar and the floor beam. Be sure to use a good wood glue and CLAMPS! If done properly, a glued joint can be stronger than the wood itself. If you don't glue the struts, repeated firing will snap the dowels. But if that happens, you can always replace them with 2-1/2" long 5/16" steel bolts.

This is also a good time to install the short struts. Glue them in place as in fig. 27.

Fig. 26.

Fig. 27

To finish the arm, you'll need all the spoon pieces. They go together like this:
(Be sure to use good gluing technique!)

 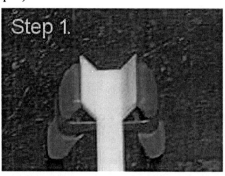 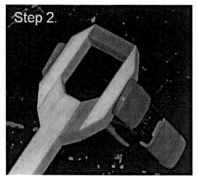

Once the glue dries and the arm's spoon is solid, we need to make a pouch for it. You can weave a pouch any way you like in the spoon, but the important thing is that the weave MUST come to the front of the spoon at the TOP, and it MUST be at the back of the spoon at the bottom. Here's a picture (fig. 29).

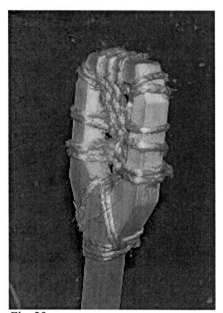

Fig. 29

If you don't construct your pouch this way, you won't get very good performance. It works a lot like a lacrosse stick.

You can weave it any way you like, but if you're not sure how to start, try this- wind the twine around the edges of the spoon like this:

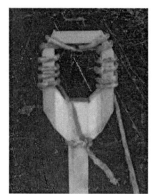

Fig. 30

Then weave the twine back and forth through the loops as in fig. 31. Finally, weave the twine up and down the lattice as in fig. 32. Don't be afraid to experiment and find a weave that you like.

Fig. 31

Fig. 32

3. The Bow.

Installing the bow is both the easiest and the hardest thing to do. The hard part is getting the bowstring on the steel bow. If you know how to do this, do it now. If you don't know how to string a bow, be careful not to bend the bow the wrong way. You're going to have to use a lot of force to get the string on, and if you apply that force to the bow the wrong way, you could damage it or make one side less powerful than the other side.

The bow should be supported in the middle and on the ends only. This way it can balance itself. Find something that you can use for leverage, like the leg of a chair perhaps. We used the end of our chop-saw table. Install the ends on the bowstring, and then install the ends onto the bow. Make sure you can slide the bow off the end of your leverage tool. We had to disassemble the table to get this one off!

Fig. 33

Once the bowstring is installed on the bow, just slide the arm of the catapult into the bow, and seat the bow in the nook of the main spar, as in fig. 34. Fig 35 shows it from the rear. The arm must be inside the bowstring or you'll never get it there when the bow is secured.

Then screw the bow anchor onto the front of the machine, in between the extended parts of the long struts. Don't glue it because you might need to remove the bow at some point in the future.

Fig. 34

Fig. 35

Fig. 36

You can also install the wheels now. Just insert the axles through the axle holes, and put the wheels onto the axles. A little dab of glue will hold them on securely.

Using a light hammer, tap a wooden peg into all the screw holes to hide the screws. The pegs will stick out a little way. This adds character and makes the machine look more medieval.

138

4. Winching, cocking, and firing.

You should have some twine left over from the pouch weaving. We'll need some of this for the winch. First make the winch hook bar. Screw an eye-screw into the thin edge of the board, about ½ inch from the end. On the opposite thin edge, screw two of the hooks so that they are exactly ¾ of an inch apart, from the inside edge of each hook. Fig. 37 shows what it should look like from the top.

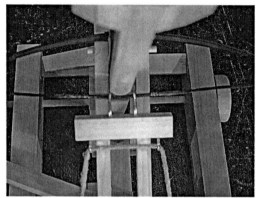
Fig. 37

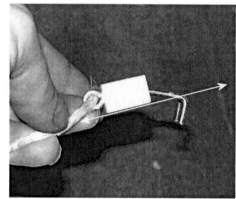
Fig. 38

The hooks should be screwed in far enough so that the threads are all inside the wood. Then they must be bent down so that the bend in the hook is slightly lower than the face of the hook bar. Fig. 38 shows this with a white line drawn parallel to the hook bar face, and the hooks bent forward. If the hooks are not bent forward enough, they will not hold the bowstring. If they are bent too far, they will be difficult to remove from the bowstring before firing.

Once the hook bar is made, install it on the machine with twine as in fig. 37 and 39. You can tie a knot in the ends of the string to keep it on the winch dowel. Screw another eye screw into the end of the trigger handle, and tie a piece of string onto it. If you have at least six feet of twine left, use that.

Fig. 39

Fig. 40

To cock the machine, first, set the trigger. Move the trigger handle all the way forward until the peg is against the floor beam. Then rotate the trigger so that it rests on top of the trigger handle.

With the winch bar hooked onto the bowstring, CHECK TO MAKE SURE THE TRIGGER IS SET! Then turn the handles and winch the bowstring down past the trigger.

Now, MAKE SURE THE TRIGGER IS SET! The arm should have pushed the trigger prop into a position so that the tip of the trigger extends up out of the space between the two long struts. If it did not, carefully push the arm down so that it props the trigger up and the bowstring will have something to hook onto. Slowly unwind the winch until the bowstring slides under the set trigger. IMPORTANT! Make sure the hooks each slide onto either side of the trigger piece. Do not let the bowstring pull the hook into the trigger, or you will damage it. If this happens, you should replace the trigger piece.

Notice how the hooks should fit easily around each edge of the trigger piece. There should be exactly ¾" of space between the hooks. Using two washers on the trigger piece gives you enough room between the trigger and the strut for the hook to pass through.

Fig 41

Once the trigger has been set, unhook the bar and lay it over behind the winch dowel. DO NOT attempt to fire the machine with the hook bar still attached to the bowstring!

Fig 42

SAFETY

When preparing to fire the machine, make sure no one is within 100 feet in front of it, or 20 feet to the sides or rear. Carefully place a golf ball or other projectile in the arm. Never attempt to launch anything weighing more than 1/2 of a pound. Step away, and pull the trigger arm back using the string attached to it. If you've done everything properly, your missile should be flying!

Expect to get about 40 to 60 feet with a golf ball. Tennis balls go about 25 feet, and baseballs about 15 to 20 feet. If you're not getting these kinds of distances, check your pouch and make sure it's not low at the top. Remember that the top of the pouch should be as far forward as possible, and the bottom should be as far back as possible.

Be sure to check your trigger for wear and tear before every firing. If you see cracks or damage that might affect the safety of the machine, do not use it! Replace the trigger first.

Also be sure to set the trigger, check to see that you set the trigger, then when you cock the machine, check again that the trigger is set! It's no fun to let go of the winch when the trigger is not set. WHACK!

Please remember that THIS CATAPULT MODEL IS NOT A TOY! It is a representative model of a real ancient military weapon and is intended to be educational. Always use under strict adult supervision, and be aware that parts of the machine can move fast enough to rip your skin open or possibly break bones. NEVER put your fingers or anything else between the arm and the strike beam or anywhere inside the bowstring and bow when cocked!

If any part of your machine is damaged or defective, do not fire the machine. Make a new parts to replace any damaged or defective parts.

This machine is capable of hurling a projectile with enough force to knock someone unconscious, break teeth and bones and rupture eyeballs. You are responsible for your own safety and the safety of others when you demonstrate this machine. PLEASE BE CAREFUL!

The Scorpion II Catapult Plans

We hope you enjoy building and shooting it as much as we've enjoyed creating it. So good luck, and have fun!

Parts list:

Wooden parts: (See drawings)	Hardware: (See next page for detailed descriptions)

1 arm 26 inches long
4 main beams 17 inches long
1 arm-channel spacer (1" x 1.25" x 2.5")
1 arm-channel spacer (1" x 1.25" x 5")
4 body-channel spacers (1" x 1" x ½")
2 linkage mount posts (4.5" long)
2 linkage-post braces 6 inches long, 45° angle cut
2 foot beams, 10 inches long, 45° angle cut
1 end cap, 3.25" x 2.5", grooved.
	Bolts: 3/8" x 5",
	     ¼" x 5" (2),
	     ¼" x 3.5",
	     ¼" x 1.5"
	Nuts: ¼" nylock (4)
	    3/8" nylock (1)
	Washers: 3/8" large (2)
	      3/8" small (2)
	Spacers: (2) small (gray)
	      (1) large (black)
	Metal Linkage bars 9.5" long (2)
	Metal Trigger bar 6.75" long
	Eye screw (4)
	6" Metal rod with eye
	Swatch of material for Pouch (1)
	Wood screws (16)
	Small metal pin (1)
	Small ring (1)
	¼" rope 12 inches long
	Length of string
	Bungee cord: 7 feet.
	Small Pulleys: 4
	1 Small Rubber Pad

Tools you will need:
1. A good wood glue. (Elmer's wood glue is recommended)
2. Two clamps capable of spanning 7 inches.
3. Wrenches to tighten the ¼" and 3/8" nuts and bolts
4. A Phillips head screwdriver
5. A light hammer
6. Scissors

Hardware: You'll be able to get most of this stuff from any hardware store. Other things you might be able to find around the house or on-line.

(2) Metal (aluminum) Linkage bars 9.5" long (see drawings)
(1) Metal (aluminum) Trigger bar 6.75" long   (see drawings)
(1) 6" Metal rod with eye (see drawings)

1 swatch of sling material – can be anything that's flexible and non-stretchy. Like denim, suede or soft leather (pig or goat leather works well) or nylon sheeting- especially the kind used for shade cloth. You'll need a finished size of 2.5" x 6" for your sling.

15 feet of twine – nylon mason's twine or hemp twine work best. Kite string is also fine.

Bolts: (1) 3/8" x 5"
        (2) ¼" x 5"
        (1) ¼" x 3.5",
        (1) ¼" x 1.5"

Nuts: (4) ¼" nylock
       (1) 3/8" nylock

Washers: (2) 3/8" ("fender" type washer – outside diameter 1.5")
         (2) 3/8" (ordinary washer – 1 inch outside diameter)

Spacers: (2) small nylon or plastic spacer (¼" inside diameter, ½" outside diameter, ½" long)
         (1) large nylon or plastic spacer (¼" inside diameter, 3/4" outside diameter, 1" long)

(4) Eye screws – inside diameter 3/16", outside diameter 3/8" about ½" of threads.

(16) Wood screws - Number 6 size, 1-5/8" long. (drywall or deck screws work well)

(1) Small metal pin - 3/16" diameter by 2" long. Brass or steel. Do not use a coat hanger wire!

(1) Small ring - ½" inside diameter, welded steel ring.

¼" rope 12 inches long – nylon or soft polyester rope works best.

Length of string (to pull the trigger with - about six to ten feet should be plenty)

3/8" diameter, heavy duty Bungee cord: 7 feet.

(4) Small sheaves (also called pulleys) McMaster.com part number 3542T81 is ideal.
    (Nylon Sheave for ½" Fibrous Rope, No Bearing, 1/4" bore, 1.875" OD)

(1) Small Rubber Pad, 1 inch square. The arm will strike this pad when firing, so the thicker the better.

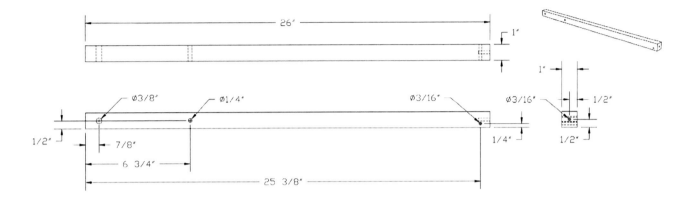

Throwing Arm (1 needed)

Lower Base Beam (2 needed)

144

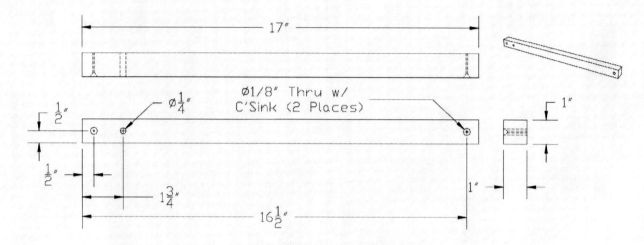

Upper Base Beam (2 needed)

17"

Ø1/8" Thru w/ C'Sink (2 Places)

Ø1/4"

1/2"

1/2"

1³/₄"

16¹/₂"

1"

1"

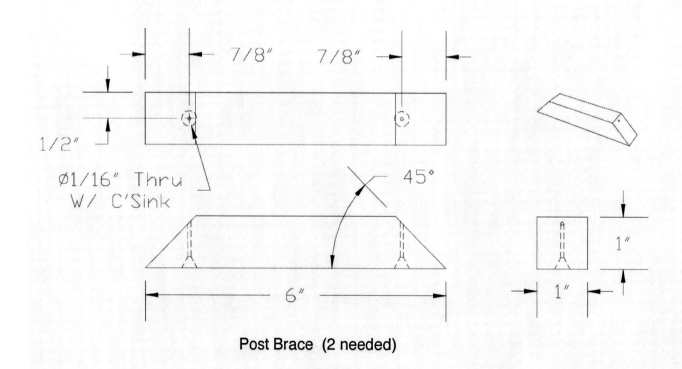

Post Brace (2 needed)

7/8"   7/8"

1/2"

Ø1/16" Thru W/ C'Sink

45°

6"

1"

1"

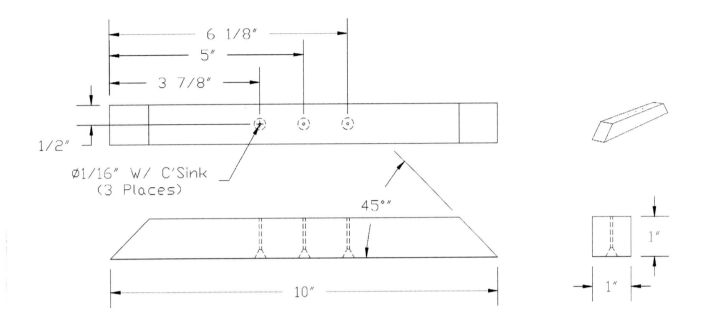

6 1/8"
5"
3 7/8"
1/2"

Ø1/16" W/ C'Sink
(3 Places)

45°"

10"

1"

1"

Foot Beam (2 needed)

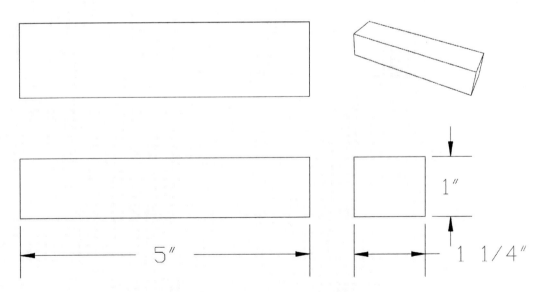

5"

1"

1 1/4"

Tall Arm Channel Spacer (1 needed)

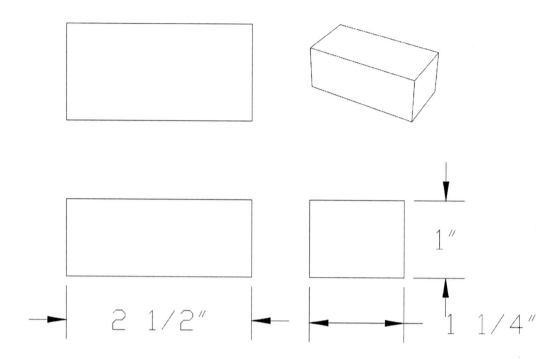

Short Arm Channel Spacer (1 needed)

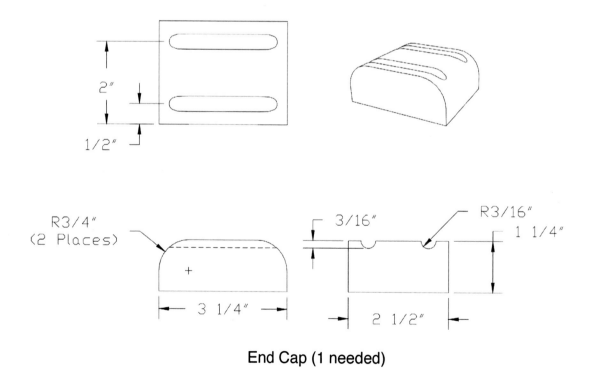

End Cap (1 needed)

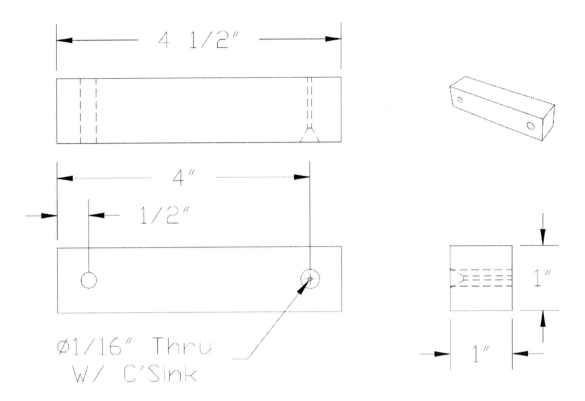

4 1/2"

4"

1/2"

Ø1/16" Thru
W/ C'Sink

1"

1"

Linkage Mount Post (2 needed)

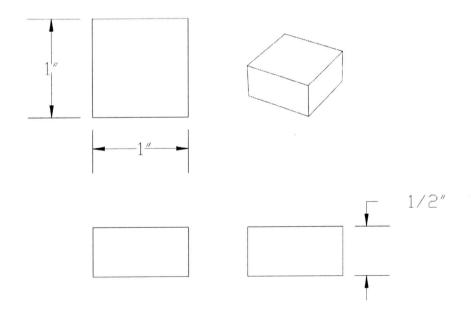

1"

1"

1/2"

Body Channel Spacers (4 needed)

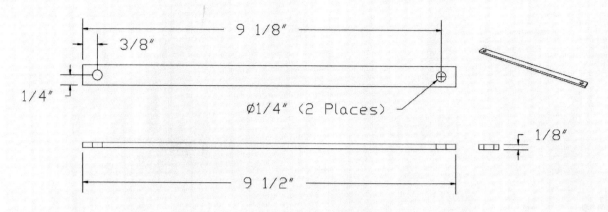

Aluminum Linkage Bar (2 needed)

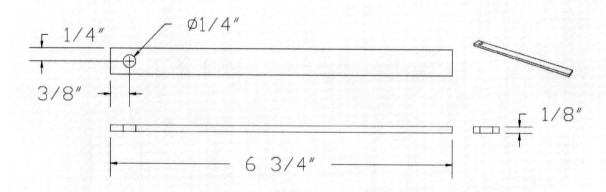

Aluminum Trigger Bar (1 needed)

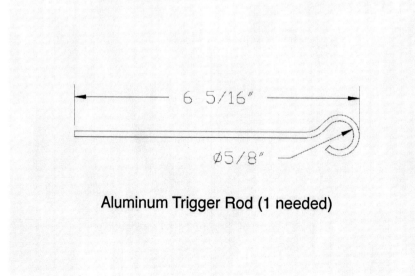

Aluminum Trigger Rod (1 needed)

:

Building the frame:

Start with the four main beams and 4 body channel spacers as in fig. 1. Make sure the large ¼" holes are on the sides and on the same end for both pieces, and each assembly should have one piece with two tiny holes near the ends. Glue them together as in fig. 2.

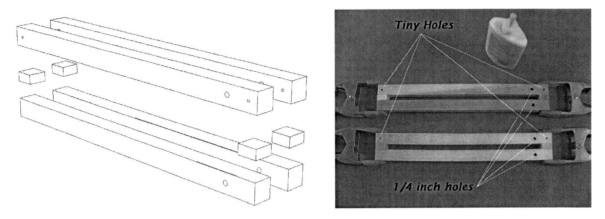

Fig 1.   Fig 2.

Get the two arm channel spacers and glue them in-between the main beams as in figs. 3 and 4. The tall spacer should go on the end away from the ¼" holes. Make sure they are both flush with the ends and the bottom of the main beams. IMPORTANT! The arm channel sides MUST be 1.25 inches apart, NOT 1 inch. Make sure you glue the spacers in wide-ways, and that the arm has good clearance (not touching the sides.)

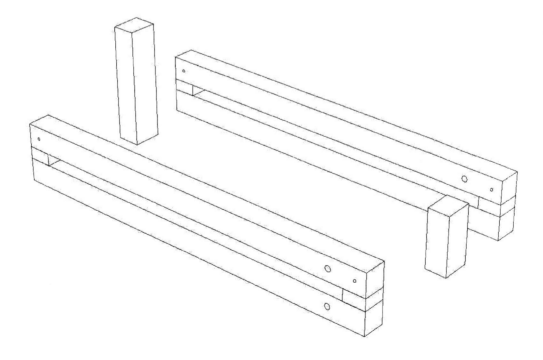

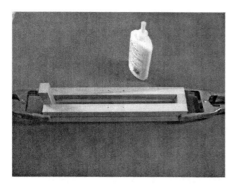

Fig 3.

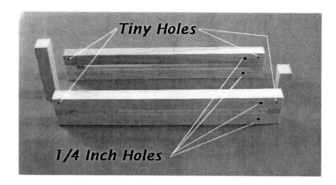

Fig 4.

The tiny holes are pilot holes for the wood screws. Screw the frame together with the screws as in fig. 5 for extra strength. Then turn the model upside down to attach the feet (fig. 6).

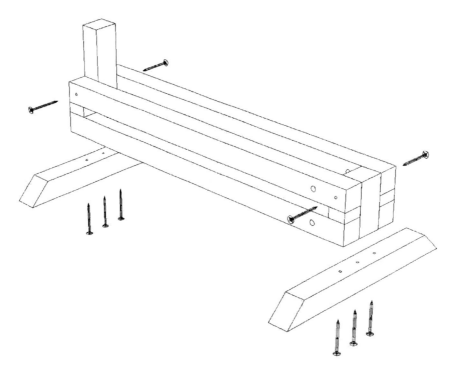

Fig 5.

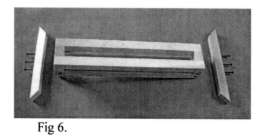

Fig 6.

Screw the feet into the frame with six of the wood screws as in fig. 7, then turn the machine upright.

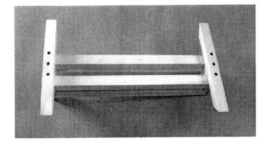

Fig 7

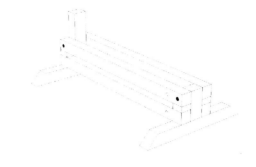

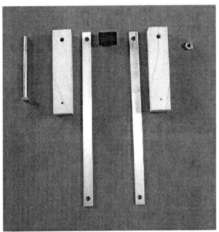

Fig 8

Fig 9

Assemble the linkage as in figs. 8 and 9. Use the 3 ½" long ¼" bolt and put it through the wooden linkage post, then one aluminum bar, then the large spacer, then the other aluminum bar, then the other linkage post. Use the locking nut to secure the assembly. Don't over tighten it- the aluminum bars should be able to rotate freely on the bolt, so be sure to leave it a little bit loose. The locking nut will not come off.

Attach the linkage assembly to the frame by gluing the linkage posts to the tall arm-channel spacer, as in fig.10. Then use two of the black screws to strengthen it (fig 11). The assembly should be flush in the front.

Fig. 10

Fig 11.

...od screws to attach the struts to the linkage posts as in figs. 12 and 13

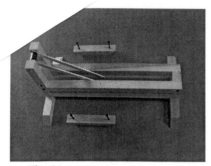

Fig. 12

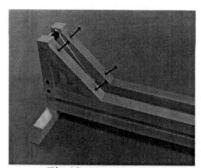

Fig 13.

Glue the end cap in place as in fig 14 and the frame is complete!

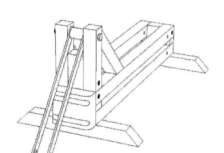

Fig 14

The Hardware:

Get the 4 pulleys and the long bolts and two locking nuts (fig 15). Insert the bolt so that there is one pulley on each side of the machine, on each of the two frame beams (figs. 16, 17). Washers are not required. Be sure to leave the nut loose enough so that the pulleys can spin freely without binding. The ¼" nut is a self-securing nut, so it will not come off even if it is not tightened all the way down.

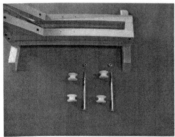

Fig 15

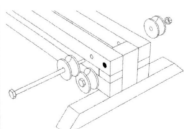

Fig 16

Fig 17

Use a light hammer to tap the metal pin into the end of the arm as in fig. 18. The pin should stick out between ¾ of an inch to one inch. The arm will attach to the frame by means of a sliding axle and the linkages we installed earlier. Put a small washer, then the small spacer, then the large washer on the long 3/8" bolt, slide it through the main channel and into the end of the arm so that the arm is centered in the frame. Then put the large washer, the spacer the small washer and the nut on the other end of the bolt. Be sure the nut is loose enough to allow the arm and axle to slide freely back and forth down the channel. With the arm in this position (laying across the linkage post spacer with the axle near the pulleys) the off-center hole in the end of the arm should be towards the top. If it is not, take the arm off and flip it over so the hole is near the top.

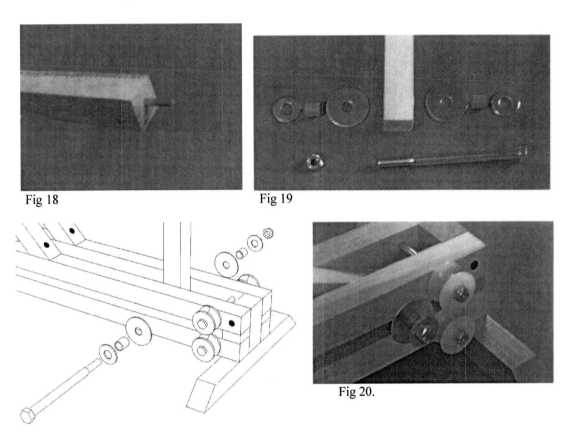

Fig 18

Fig 19

Fig 20.

Attach the arm to the linkages with the 1.5" long bolt and a lock nut (fig 21). Once again, the nut should be loose enough to allow the linkages to rotate freely on the bolt. There should be no resistance when the arm is moved back and forth.

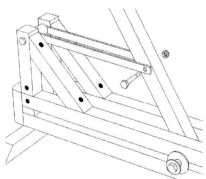

Fig 21

Fig 22

...e eye-screws into the end of the frame near the pulleys. It should be centered in the end of ...e beam as in fig. 23. Tie a strong knot in one end of the ¼" rope. A figure 8 knot is a great ... You should melt the end of the rope into a button so it can't come untied. Then thread the rope ...rough the eye screw as in fig. 24.

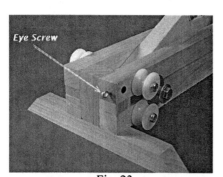

Eye Screw

Fig. 23

Figure 8 knot.

Fig 24

Bring the arm back so that it rests in the cocked position. Pull the rope over the arm and thread the loose end through the hole in the aluminum trigger bar. Take out the slack, and tie another strong knot in the rope at the trigger bar as in figs. 25 and 26. Cut off the excess rope and melt the end into a button.

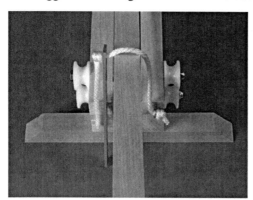

Fig 25.

Fig. 26

Now screw two of the eye screws into the top of the frame opposite the rope attachment (fig. 27). One screw should be one inch from the back of the machine, and the other should be 4 inches from the back (3 inches from the first screw). See fig; 28. Then insert the eye-rod into the eye-screws as in fig.28

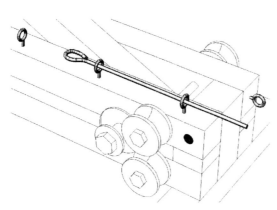

Fig 27

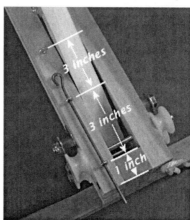

3 inches

3 inches

1 inch

Fig 28

With the eye-rod inserted, screw the last eye-screw into the frame 7 inches from the end (3 inches from the middle eye-screw) as in fig. 28. Now tie a 5 foot long (or longer) piece of string to the eye-rod and thread it through the last eye screw. The trigger is complete.

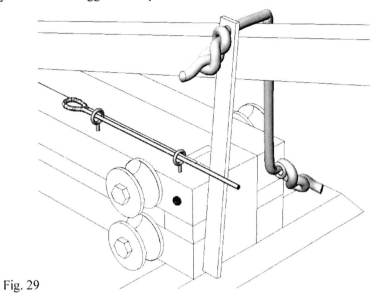

Fig. 29

Now take the bungee cord and tie it into a loop. Use a simple square knot, and pull it tight (fig. 30, 31).

Fig 30

Fig 31

Install the bungee onto the frame as in figs. 32 and 33. The knot should be positioned so it doesn't get in the way of any moving parts.

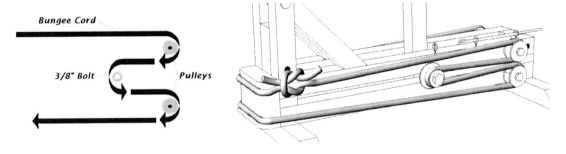

Fig 32

Fig 33.

The Sling.

Cut a piece of the sling pouch material about 6" x 6" and lay it flat. Fold two sides over so they touch in the center as below, making a strip 6" x 3" double thick (**A**). Then fold the edges of this strip (lengthwise) up (**B**), then in half back down (**C**) to form an 'M' shape. Turn this over so the 'M' is now a 'W' (**D**).

Tie each end tight with the twine about ¾" from each end of the sling pouch so that the knot is on the top of the 'W', then push the center of the 'W' inside out (through the bottom) and you should be left with a perfect sling-pouch.

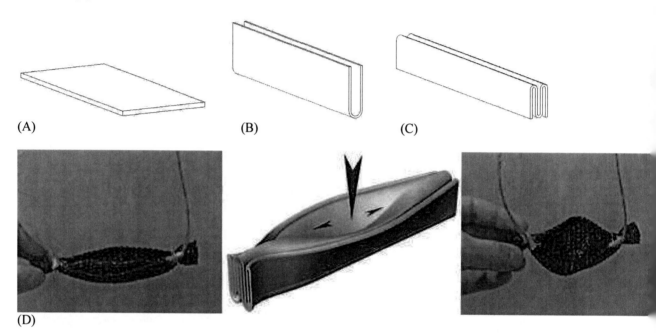

(A)   (B)   (C)

(D)

Make sure that the sling-pouch cradles the ball so that it won't easily slip out, but not too deep or the ball won't come out at all. The pouch should just barely cradle the ball.

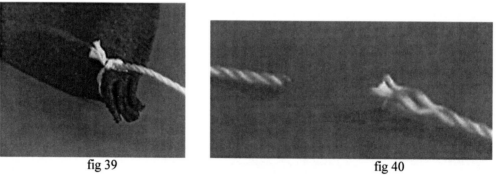

fig 39   fig 40

Fusing:

Fusing is a technique used on nylon and poly ropes to melt the end of the string and prevent it from unraveling. You can even melt the end into a small button making it almost impossible to slip through a knot. In the photo (Fig. 40), the end on the right is not fused, but the end on the left is. Do this by holding the end near a small flame just until it begins to melt. But don't catch the string on fire!

On one end of the sling-pouch, cut the string about 12 inches long and tie a loop in the end. Then slide the loop through and over the steel ring so that the ring is 8 inches from the pouch (It's ok if it's a little bit over 8 inches, we'll tell you how to shorten it later). Your finished pouch should look like fig. 45, but longer.

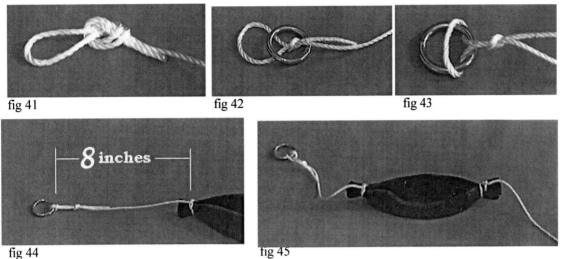

fig 41   fig 42   fig 43

fig 44   fig 45

On the other end of the sling, cut the string about 15 inches long. This end will attach to the arm.

Tie a knot in the long sling string so that the knot is the same length from the pouch as the steel ring is on the other string, about 8 inches. Use this knot as a marker to know where to tie it to the arm. With the arm in the UN-COCKED position, thread the long string through the hole in the arm, tie and fuse the end of the string so that the marker knot is just on the top of the arm, as in fig 46.

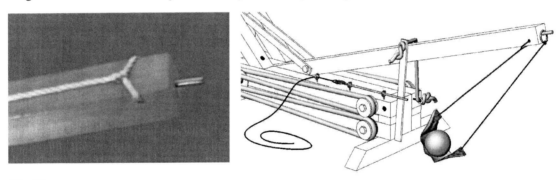

Fig 46.

Fig 47.

Cocking and firing the machine:

To cock the machine, secure the Scorpion to the ground somehow- we use tent stakes to hold ours in place. Pull the arm up and over, stretching the bungee until the arm is all the way back, as in fig. 47.. NEVER stand with your head or any part of your body over the arm! Hold it down and slide the eye-rod so that it sticks out the back of the machine as far as possible. Place the trigger string and aluminum bar over the arm and hook the aluminum bar behind the rod as in fig. 47. You may need help with this step. You now have a live machine, so be careful! Note that there is no safety mechanism built in to the machine. This trigger is very sensitive, so DO NOT cock the machine until you are ready to fire it. Once cocked and loaded, get up and move away from the machine.

Situate the sling pouch as in fig 48. Make sure there is nothing for 300 feet in front of the machine and 100 feet behind it. Place a golf ball or tennis ball in the sling pouch and stand at least 6 feet off to the side. Let everyone in the area know what's about to happen, stand off to the side and gently pull the line…

Fig 48.

Tuning:

You can tune the machine by shortening or lengthening the sling. Just tie knots in the string to make it shorter. Each knot will take about ¼ of an inch out of the length. To make it longer, just untie some of the knots. You can also shorten or lengthen the bungee cord to change the power by adjusting the knots in it.

Don't expect the same performance with tennis balls and golf balls. Different projectiles will have different ranges and achieve different heights due to their weight and aerodynamic qualities. In our tests with this model, golf balls go about 300 feet, and tennis balls go about 120 feet.

Safety:

Please remember that THIS CATAPULT MODEL IS NOT A TOY! It is a working model of a real mechanical hurling machine and is intended to be educational. Always use under strict adult supervision, and be aware that the pin on the end of the arm moves fast enough to rip your skin open, and the arm moves fast enough to potentially break bones. NEVER put your fingers, arms, face or anything else in the path of the arm!

If any part of your machine is damaged or defective, do not fire the machine!

This machine is capable of hurling a projectile with enough force to knock someone unconscious, break teeth and bones and rupture eyeballs. You are responsible for your own safety and the safety of others when you demonstrate this machine. PLEASE BE CAREFUL!

Section Four:
Going Farther

Other kinds of catapults:

There are many types of Catapults. In modern times, the word catapult can be used to describe any machine that hurls a projectile. This can include a slingshot used to hurl pebbles, a machine that launches airplanes off aircraft carriers, a compressed air powered cannon, and of course, the ancient weapons of smash destruction!

Every year, during the first weekend of November in rural Delaware there is a competition of hurling devices known as "Punkin Chunkin". The Annual Punkin Chunkin competition has been the place to be for hurling enthusiasts of all ages for more than three decades, and doesn't seem to be slowing down. If you go there, you'll see lots of different types of counterweight driven Trebuchets, Torsion and tension powered devices, machines powered by tuck engines and others by compressed air tanks.

Punkin Chunkin is by far the largest and oldest of the modern hurling competitions, but it is not the first, and it's not the only one either. There have been major hurling competitions in the US going back to 1966, and if you look hard enough, you'll find lots of them around the country today, including a nationwide school-based competition called "Storm the Castle" as pat of the Science Olympiad.

If you go to any of the larger competitions, you'll see a lot of machines that don't fit into any category within the earlier part of this book, including air cannons and centrifugal machines.

The compressed air cannons are the "big guns" at the shows. They typically propel an eight to ten pound pumpkin anywhere from 2000 feet to 4000 feet. If they try to shoot farther than that, the velocity of the pumpkins begins to approach the speed of sound and the massive air friction causes the vegetable to splatter in mid-air, producing an effect known as "pie in the sky". However, bowling balls can easily be shot over a mile by these extremely powerful machines.

The big air cannons use the same principles as a spud gun, just on a much larger scale. The spud guns are quite dangerous, some are able to propel a potato right through a car door. The US Air Force uses a version of a spud gun to shoot frozen chickens at airplane windshields to simulate a bird strike at supersonic speeds. Since these are high pressure vessels which can explode without warning, it is not wise to experiment with them unless you are a professional engineer.

Other types of catapults you might see at a hurling festival are the centrifugal machines. They typically use a truck engine to turn a long arm mounted to the top of a tower. When it gets spinning fast enough, a pumpkin is released from the end of the arm. The challenge is to release it at just the right time, and to design a tower and arm that won't disintegrate when it suddenly becomes imbalanced (by losing nine or ten pounds off one end) while rotating at full speed.

Next in the power spectrum are the torsion and tension machines. Take a trebuchet and replace the counterweight with springs attached between the end of the arm and the lower part of the frame, and you've got a tension machine. An American sling shot is also a tension device. The Onager and Ballista models in this book are torsion machines, and the Scorpion and Petraria are tension machines.

In the competitions, torsion machines can usually outperform the trebuchets for distance, but only when hurling a ten pound missile. Large trebuchets can easily launch hundreds of pounds into the air and hundreds of feet down range. And it's the trebuchets that exhibit the greatest diversity of design in hurling competitions around the world.

When I invented the Floating Arm Trebuchet (FAT) in 1999, it was partly an academic experiment to see if I could improve on the efficiency of what is generally considered the most efficient projectile throwing device in history - the medieval counterweight trebuchet, and partly it was an attempt to make something new and different for a TV show I had been asked to participate in.

The FAT did both those things, but more importantly (and to my surprise), it inspired hundreds of imitators world wide, and spurred more innovation by students and hobbyists who were intent on hurling their projectiles farther, higher and faster with their own new designs. These designs incorporated such innovations as arms rolling over cams, jointed arms, multi-rotational arms, floating everything, and every combination of those concepts you can imagine. They've all been tried. If you search for some of these acronyms and names on-line, you can find out more about them: AROC, AROW, FET, FAW, FEKA, Golf Ball Whipper, King Arthur Treb, and that's just a start. There's also a very good message board at www.TheHurl.org where new designs and old ones are continuously being discussed and improved.

Why should a kid build a catapult?

Because the world needs good engineers and scientists, and because the kids who will grow up to become engineers and scientists need a way to get hands-on experience with physics, math and engineering.

Energy can neither be created nor destroyed. That's one of the fundamental principles of modern physics, and it's an important one for everyone to understand. It affects how we think of things like fossil fuels, food production (food is the energy source for your body), city planning, global warming and much more. Weather patterns can be explained as large energy systems, and in the 1960s at least one highly respected scientist suggested ways to control weather patterns with atmospheric atomic blasts (fortunately, the politics didn't quite work out.) For a kid building a trebuchet, and calculating the efficiency of energy in vs. energy out, the law of conservation of energy becomes obvious in a real and tangible way that can't be achieved by just reading a book.

In this age of 200-plus channels of TV, the Internet and computer games, kids are also spending far less time building tree houses, tinkering with engines, or designing downhill racers. We believe those are important skills to have. They help form the basis for good problem solving skills and an innate understanding of the real, physical world that you just can't get from a computer game, no matter how good its physics simulation software is.

Ballistic motion was one of the key players in the development of the science of physics. Even the word "engineer" originated as the builders and designers of Siege Engines in the middle ages.

Why is a budding engineering student expected to take a year or two of calculus in high school, but she isn't expected to have any real-world experience in building or working with machines and materials? Pencil and paper and computer screens are only one part of the learning experience. Where will she apply all of the stuff she learned in geometry and trig? Without physical projects to touch, feel and see, the lessons become abstract, their utility questionable.

A catapult project gives students a chance to see that science and engineering really can be fun, and it's a lot more than just numbers on paper. The real payoff for an engineer is in the field, where she can see and enjoy the results of her ingenuity. And it may seem counterintuitive, but engineering projects not only help kids learn math and science, they are also great at getting kids back outdoors, away from the massive over-exposure to video games, TV and the Internet.

Why all this interest in getting kids to study science and engineering? Because it's important to our society, and it's great mental cross training regardless of what field of work the kids eventually go into. Most people develop a sense for what they want to do in life while they are still in high school or even earlier. A catapult project is fun and interesting enough to inspire some kids to study the science behind how they work, and then go on to become the engineers and scientists of tomorrow.

CPSIA information can be obtained at www.ICGtesting.com
Printed in the USA
BVOW04s1530180416

444388BV00020B/90/P